THE GEEK LEADER'S HANDBOOK

THE GEEK LEADER'S HANDBOOK

Essential Leadership Insight for
People with Technical Backgrounds

PAUL GLEN AND MARIA MCMANUS

The Geek Leader's Handbook

Essential Leadership Insight for People with Technical Backgrounds

Printed in the United States of America

Published by Leading Geeks Press

3253 Malcolm Avenue

Los Angeles, CA 90034

Phone: 310-694-0450

ISBN 978-0-9712468-2-9

To the memory of
William Lewis Brown
and
Peggy Ann Carlisle McManus

TABLE OF CONTENTS

INTRODUCTION

If you've ever wondered why on earth you took on a management role, when all you really wanted to do was write code, *The Geek Leader's Handbook* is for you. If you've ever questioned how you are supposed to represent your team when the leaders of all those other departments are so unreasonable and unpredictable, this is your book. If you've ever wished you could get real, meaningful advice that speaks to your most pressing questions about leadership, you've found the book you need.

Nearly every leadership book we've read speaks to general audiences about generic leadership principles. We wanted to target our advice and speak only to leaders who have risen through the ranks of technical work. Generic doesn't cut it for them. They have been trained in creating flawless technology, a discipline that requires right answers, unimpeachable logic, and thorough risk assessment. It admits little of the gray shadings that permeate much of life. As such, they are often underprepared for the ambiguities of leading teams and representing them in the larger organization.

The two of us feel that, as a team, we provide insight you're not likely to find anywhere else. When a geek who is an award-winning author joins forces with a decidedly non-geek expert on user experience, you are going to get a new – and valuable – perspective. We've delved deeply into what makes geeks a breed apart and how the strengths and proclivities that make for excellence in creating technology can often leave geeks at sea when leading teams and dealing with non-geek leaders.

We're confident that you'll find this advice practically applicable and thought-provoking, whether you are:

- An experienced manager looking to up your game
- A relatively new manager trying to figure things out
- A technical contributor considering a move into management
- A non-technical manager suddenly faced with leading a technical group

And you will be comforted to know that just about every technical leader faces similar leadership challenges. Here's why:

No one gets trained to do this. Most technical leaders come from a technical background. They are trained in the disciplines of technology, not of management.

Traditional management training doesn't work that well for geeks. Most management training programs, whether academic or commercial, are focused on generic techniques of management and leadership. They don't account for the nature of the people being led or the work being done. But we all know that geeks are not run-of-the-mill people. They are a special breed. And their work is fundamentally different from most other work.

You need to transcend your history. The habits of thought and work instilled by technical training and practice, problem-solving, and analysis often serve as a straitjacket for managers who come up as technologists. The habits and assumptions that made you so successful as an individual contributor – the very things that got you the leadership job in the first place – may undermine your ability to perform in that role.

This book is designed to help you overcome these challenges as quickly as possible by leveraging the experience of many of those who have gone before you. You'll find a combination of immediately applicable techniques and foundational insights drawn from research and experience.

Each chapter covers a single, focused topic of concern to new and experienced technical leaders. In fact, each one originally stood alone as a white paper requested and distributed by our partners at Citrix. Together, we have identified themes that are common to many managers who come from a technical background. In these explicit situations, we have uncovered surprising insights and tips that mainstream leadership advice overlooks. And we've done this the hard way. By examining our own contrasting worldviews, biases, and assumptions, we have unearthed a wealth of unexpected and practical advice to help leaders who have technical backgrounds succeed as leaders.

Paul's previous book, *Leading Geeks: How to Manage and Lead People Who Deliver Technology*, helped to reveal the unique nature of geeks and geek leadership. Our hope is that this book will help you become a more confident and effective leader by uncovering the precarious relationship between geeks and non-geeks and offering you pragmatic advice on how to manage your relationships with both.

~ Paul Glen and Maria McManus, Los Angeles, California, 2014

PART I

GEEK LEADERSHIP

ARCHETYPES, NOT STEREOTYPES

Throughout this book we refer to geeks, affectionately and advisedly. Our definition of a geek is:

> **geek** *noun; slang.* An expert or enthusiast in an analytical field such as computers or engineering. At one time considered an insult, it has become a badge of honor for technical people.

We also frequently contrast geeks with non-geeks. The labels might seem like gratuitous stereotyping, but we recognize that every person is an individual, and we do not mean for the traits we refer to to be descriptive in an absolute way. Men tend to be taller than women; that doesn't preclude there being tall women and short men. Similarly, people who work in technology tend to be analytical, preferring objectively verifiable truth over personal experience; that doesn't mean that all people with technical backgrounds share that preference. When we describe geeks, we are referring to trends and patterns that are readily observable, but by no means absolute.

We set up archetypes of geeks and non-geeks to make it easier to recognize patterns that appear in work relationships. We find that this actually helps people to be more accommodating of individual differences, because it makes differences understandable instead of threatening. When we can't see into the inner lives of people who are different from us, we tend to dismiss them. But when we get a glimpse of the inner lives of people who are different from us, we are better able to relate to their hopes, dreams, fears, and dreads and more inclined to make allowances for their differences.

This ability is a fundamental aspect of leadership, and it's not something you are likely to have been taught in your technical training. So read on, and when you see us referring to geeks and non-geeks, remember that we are referencing archetypes, not stereotypes.

CONTRAXIOMS: A CONCEPTUAL FRAMEWORK

Our reason for writing this book is to offer you practical, immediately applicable advice about how to lead technical people. But all good advice emerges from a solid framework for understanding the problem. In this chapter, we invite you to explore the ideas and insights from which this leadership advice grew.

The framework came from three distinct sources:

- Reflections on our personal work experiences

- Academic research

- A rich, ongoing conversation that we will share with you in this chapter

If you are in the midst of a crisis or simply feel eager to get to the "what to do" sections of the book, feel free to skip over this chapter. Each chapter stands alone, summarizing and repeating important concepts when necessary, so you won't be disoriented if you choose to skip around. That said, we encourage you to come back to this chapter later, because we believe the benefits of its insights extend beyond the limits of work life.

Not only will this chapter give you a deeper understanding of the advice that follows and how to adapt it to your own situation, but you also might just learn some important things about yourself and the people around you. In fact, as we've presented these ideas to audiences around the country for several years, we've been surprised by how many people have excitedly told us that these ideas had the potential to transform their relationships with family, friends, and neighbors, and not just work colleagues.

THE SOURCE OF THE PROBLEM

What is it about some people that drives us so crazy?

Maybe the person is the chatterbox in the cube by the window. Maybe it's your negligent boss. Maybe it's that smarmy, glad-handing sales guy. Maybe it's the ignorant, irrational stakeholder with way more power than she deserves. Maybe it's those robotic, condescending jerks who can never meet a deadline. We're just getting warmed up here. If we were to really capture the simmering rage that permeates many workplaces, we'd need several hundred more pages.

But for our purposes we need only ask you to recall the many instances of righteous indignation you've experienced at work in response to people who just didn't do what they were supposed to do. Our hope in writing this chapter is not that you will dwell on these negative feelings, but that we will help you understand where they come from and what you can do about transforming them.

We have discovered that the source of this frustration at work is neither obvious nor mysterious. There are patterns in our emotional reactions at work, especially between geeks and non-geeks. These patterns are hidden behind the routine disappointments and petty misunderstandings of daily work life. When you become aware of these patterns, you will find a new freedom to interrupt and transform your habitual response to them, thereby achieving a more positive outcome for yourself, your team, your colleagues, and your organization.

So the next time your client dithers about signing off on requirements, you will have a new tool to understand his perspective and your knee-jerk response to it. You will then have a larger menu of responses from which to choose for how you want to handle the situation. With this information, you can form hypotheses and make predictions about your own emotional life at work, and experience a new sense of insight, control, and even hope.

A NEW WORD

We have discovered a tool for making sense of discord at work.

It is a word.

It is a word that emerged from our experience, as a geek and a non-geek, trying to work together to understand why it is so hard to work together. We discovered that we needed this new word after more than a year of reviewing the social science literature about geek/non-geek relationship problems. We had read, categorized, and synthesized scores of articles on neuroscience, psychology, organizational culture, management, and leadership, looking for clues.

Meanwhile, in working together, we had many minor but exasperating misunderstandings of our own. Minor incidents that were microcosms of the frustrations that we had experienced in our careers. Paul relived his frustrations of working with "the business" – too emotional, flighty, and unpredictable. Maria relived her frustrations of working with technical teams – too aloof, dispassionate, noncommittal, and obsessed with details. We used each aggravation as an opportunity. We dissected and parsed and tested each disturbance and learned from it.

We realized that at some level, we geeks and non-geeks had entirely different worldviews. We saw the same physical universe around us but understood it in remarkably different ways. And our different understandings led us to judge each other, often harshly.

But more importantly, acting as representatives of our tribes, we found what seems to be the source of these different worldviews:

We have fundamentally different assumptions about how the world works and how it should work, assumptions about what we think of as right and wrong, what is true and false, and even about how people should be in the world.

As we discerned this phenomenon again and again, we struggled to talk about it, because we could find no name for it. We puzzled over this for days until one afternoon, Paul said:

"If we were talking about math, I'd call these assumptions axioms, truths so fundamental that they are presumed as foundational rather than proved."

"And we have very different axioms, conflicted and contrasting," added Maria.

After a few moments of silent contemplation, "Contraxioms!" offered Maria.

We had a name!

And then Paul came up with an elegantly phrased definition:

Contraxiom *noun*. A matched pair of contrasting axioms that give rise to vastly different worldviews.

And immediately we realized that we had found a way to talk about a phenomenon at the heart of the geek/non-geek divide and a word whose time had come.

FROM IDEA TO APPLICATION

Once we had a word to capture and communicate the idea, we started to recognize contraxioms at play wherever we looked, and not just between geeks and non-geeks.

You've probably seen it at Thanksgiving dinner, when you have to button your lip while your uncle who watches the wrong (to your mind) news channel delivers his annual diatribe. One of you fervently believes that government is evil and incompetent. The other fervently believes that government is essential to protect people from one another's predatory instincts.

You see contraxioms at play in marriages, where one wants to talk about how her argument with her boss made her feel, while the other just wants to solve the problem and move on. *She* believes that when someone listens to her emotions she will feel better, while *he* believes that she will feel better when the circumstance that caused the pain are resolved.

You see them in the workplace when a CFO believes that the right way for the company to become profitable is by cutting expenses. The sales director believes that profits will flow from a boost in sales. They argue bitterly over the expensive gifts lavished on clients.

Underlying all these conflicts, and fueling the outrage associated with them, are contrasting axioms, unarticulated and unquestioned beliefs about how the world *should* work and how people *should* behave. And because these beliefs are taken as true, they become as invisible and ubiquitous as the air we breathe, the backdrop for our everyday existence.

When people share our fundamental assumptions, we know we belong and feel comfortable together because we feel understood and accepted. When people don't share these assumptions, and their activities are evidence of it, we recognize that they don't belong. This is the beginning of "us and them." These hidden axioms are what we use to determine who is in and who is out.

At core, humans are tribal beings. Whether we consider someone to be in our tribe or not – friend or foe – triggers powerful instincts about how we should treat them. Some fascinating emerging research in brain science is demonstrating that we think of people who are not part of our tribe as somewhat less human, less deserving of our first-tier moral sensibility, less deserving of our support, compassion, and understanding.

Yet exposing the contraxioms that separate us is helpful in reducing tensions, improving communication, and smoothing collaboration. Two groups need not share all the same assumptions to share goals and work together. They do not have to pretend that differences don't exist or repress their outrage at each other. In fact, understanding others' contraxioms reduces outrage, because "those people" become less mysterious and more predictable. Their different assumptions become less a violation of our contraxioms and more a source of diversity in perspective. In short, they become more human to us.

Understanding the nature of the contraxioms that separate geeks and non-geeks is a new and promising opportunity to bridge the divide that has been an obstacle to progress (and happiness) at work for decades.

THE 7 CONTRAXIOMS OF GEEKS AND NON-GEEKS

After several years of exploring this, we have found seven contraxioms that separate geeks and non-geeks and give rise to a significant amount of dysfunction when we try to work together.

We have different ideas of what *work* is.

We relate to the *future* in vastly different ways.

We come to *know* what we know very differently.

We have very different ideas about the purpose of *language*.

We disagree about the definition and significance of *lying*.

We see *good and evil* with different degrees of absolutism.

We value *desire* and its role in decision-making differently.

On first reading, these things may seem rather abstract and academic, unlikely to be useful in the hurly-burly of work life, but we assure you that they are at play in every meeting room and every cubicle, subtly and silently undermining projects, triggering outrage, and fostering mistrust.

We're going to briefly explain each one of these, explore how they trigger the everyday breakdowns you already experience, and what you, as a geek leader, can do to make things better.

WORK

We have different ideas of what work is.

For geeks, work is about solving problems.

For non-geeks, work is about achieving a vision.

At first glance this may seem like an inconsequential difference. You go to work and do what needs to be done. You fix the international tax algorithm in the accounting software, build a mobile app, add new fields to the customer database, and revise the monthly reports. Does it matter how you conceptualize the meaning of work?

Yes, it does. Because not understanding the differences between us undermines our ability to work together in two ways.

- We disagree about how work should be approached.

- Our conflicting approaches prevent us from planning together.

Now let's take a closer look at these differences to understand how they hold us back.

Solving problems

Geeks are problem-solving creatures. Problems and solutions organize their thinking about almost everything, but especially work. They provide a structured approach for defining goals, tasks, and progress. They give geeks the assumptions, rules, constraints, and success criteria that concentrate their attention and efforts. They offer geeks an appealing sense that there is a right answer.

Because geeks see the world through this problem-solution lens, their thinking remains firmly planted in the present. Problems only exist in the here and now, as either obstacles or opportunities. The solving of problems dictates what geeks should do at work to make progress. In other words, geeks plan for the future by starting with the present and working forward in a series of next steps.

Achieving visions

But not everyone approaches work this way. For many people, work is about achieving visions. Visions are imagined experiences in the future – beautiful, profitable, exciting dreams of how things could be. The more vividly imagined these experiences are, the more they build excitement for achieving them.

Because non-geeks see work as achieving visions, their thinking tends to be more future-oriented. They feel free to dream as broadly as their imaginations allow. The more vividly they imagine, the more explicit they can be about what needs to happen to achieve the vision. Non-geeks plan by starting with the future and working backward, in an arrangement of dependencies.

How this plays out

Let's imagine a work scenario, where it has come down from on high that your organization must increase customer loyalty. And you're the one geek who has been invited to the brainstorming meeting.

The non-geeks, in this case marketing people, start to form a vision about sending birthday greetings to customers. They start to elaborate, imagining the customer's experience of receiving the email.

"Wouldn't it be great if our customers could get a coupon from us on their birthdays, so that they could feel like they really matter to us?"

You like this idea, but wonder how it will be possible, given that the database doesn't store customers' birthdates. Your colleagues continue to explore the idea.

"Oh, and if the coupon were related to their last purchase!"

"No, that would be creepy."

"Just a straight discount would feel good, but make it for one day only so that there is some urgency."

"The email should have a picture of them, so that they know we know what they look like. It will feel more personal."

"No, the email should have a picture of our president. Definitely there should be a face, but I think it has to be from us to them."

Meanwhile, you, the geek leader, are probably considering the problem. You ask yourself, "How can we get from where we are (problem) to where we want to be (solution)?" You think:

"The problem is we can't automate sending customer greetings because we don't have their birthdates in the customer database.

"The solution will be to add a field to the customer database to store the birthday and write a program that sends greetings every night. And then we need to find a source for the data and a process for keeping it up to date."

As the problem and solution become clearer in your mind, you start to get more impatient with your colleagues' fuzzy, fantastical thinking. "What does it matter what goes in the email," you think, "if we don't even know our customers' birthdays?" So you try to focus them on what's important to you at that moment rather than those extraneous ideas. They aren't on the critical path of how to get it done – they aren't thinking like geeks – and since first things should come first, you feel the need to focus attention on the problem and its solution.

But what you don't know is that the act of vividly imagining the full experience will help your colleagues to understand the dependencies – what will need to be done in order to achieve this motivating vision. Adding the field to the database, writing the script to run each night, and populating and maintaining the data are things that will make more sense to them in the context of enabling the experience they want to create and the results they want to achieve.

And if you interrupt or invalidate their process of imagining the vision, you will lose their engagement, insights, and enthusiasm for the work. As if that weren't bad enough, you risk preventing them from articulating the requirements you need.

Inner dialogue

How geeks respond to the Work Contraxiom:

> "Your fuzzy visions are too vague to work on."

> "You get all mad whenever I try to make sense of your fantasies."

> "You refuse to break your vision into concrete pieces that I can estimate."

How non-geeks respond to the Work Contraxiom

> "You want to turn my beautiful vision into a problem."

> "Your nattering questions don't let my imagination go where it needs to."

> "You won't talk about a launch date, so I can't work backwards."

The result is that we fight about how to work rather than collaborating on the work itself.

OVERHEARD

As a product person working on the website for a media company, it was my job to envision new experiences for our customers, to engage them so they would be happy to return so we could sell ads at a premium. But it was always difficult to work with tech teams in the early phases of product development. It seemed like new ideas made them anxious, and they couldn't join in our brainstorming. They weren't comfortable talking about what we might do, and were only happy, productive participants after we nailed down the "what" so they could go tackle the how. Their impatience with our process for figuring out what we wanted to do was palpable, yet we needed them

---

> there to test the plausibility of what we were thinking. In all, it
> was very uncomfortable, and we avoided doing it.

What to do

As a geek leader, once you notice that the Work Contraxiom is interfering with your work and relationships, you have the opportunity to mitigate the frustrations and dysfunctions that result. Here are some suggestions:

- Give them time to explore their visions in vivid detail. Don't interrupt their imaginative thinking with immediate questions about implementation approaches or plausibility.

- Try to understand the experience they want to create, including how they and others will feel when this vision is achieved. This is more important than the specific requirements. If you understand the experience that they want to create, you can suggest alternative technical approaches.

- Get explicit agreement on a problem statement that will guide you and your team. Instead of asking them, "What problem do you want to solve?" synthesize what you've heard and offer up a problem statement that describes the experience they want to create, and then refine your understanding together.

> ### CATCHING A CONTRAXIOM IN THE ACT
>
> You will never see a contraxiom directly. No one is going to stand up in a meeting and say, "We fundamentally disagree about the nature and meaning of work." Contraxioms hide in

our everyday interactions and our internal thoughts and judgments of each other.

But to make best use of your knowledge of contraxioms, you need to "catch them in the act," to recognize their effects as they're happening. When you see them at play, you have the opportunity to adjust your responses to others, to reduce your stress, let go of your judgments, and access the value that different perspectives provide.

Luckily, contraxioms are not undetectable. Even if they don't reflect light, they do cast a shadow, and you can see it if you know where to look.

And the most important place to look is in your own internal thoughts and feelings as you respond to people on the other side of the divide. The best indicator that a contraxiom is at play is when you notice yourself thinking something that you'd likely never say out loud.

FUTURE

We relate to the future in vastly different ways.

For geeks, the future is looming.

For non-geeks, the future is promising.

The Future Contraxiom is about a fundamental difference in what we consider to be the correct way to think about what has not yet happened. Geeks feel responsible for assessing the looming obstacles and risks that may obstruct their plans, while non-geeks feel no such obligation and often rebuff attempts to consider risks, annoyed at the "negativity."

This difference isn't really about optimism vs. pessimism, since geeks are often spectacularly optimistic (especially when it comes to estimating the amount of work that can be done over the weekend). This contraxiom is more about the virtue of risk analysis, how it fuels creativity for geeks and kills creativity for non-geeks.

Non-geeks regularly complain that geeks are "The Department of No," that they are always eager and ready to find reasons that nothing will ever work. As a leader, you need to know where that reputation comes from, and this contraxiom can help explain it.

Looming

For geeks, the future is looming because:

1. Geeks are trained to plan for the worst.

If you don't consider all the things that could go wrong, then things break. And this is bad. Engineers who build bridges need to think about freezing temperatures, wind speed, floods, erosion, and rambunctious parades so that they can be sure that the bridge doesn't collapse. Technology leaders need to consider both technical and non-technical risks that threaten project success. They consider endless possibilities such as malicious users, component failures, usage spikes, personnel turnover, technology upgrades, and changes in business direction. In fact, they consider risk planning a sacred obligation. To not plan for risks on a project would be an abdication of professional responsibility, a form of technical malpractice.

2. Geeks hate the future.

The future is inherently unknown and unknowable. You can't see it, touch it, or taste it. Descriptions of it are ambiguous fantasies. Geeks (to speak of them as an archetype) hate ambiguity, and they hate things for which there is no possibility of proof.

3. Geeks consider the future a fantasy unless there is a clear and plausible plan to create it.

For anything in the future to feel even remotely real to geeks, they need to see a logical, plausible chain of events leading to it, and then their discomfort in talking about the future simmers down. If you come to geeks and say you want a mobile app, their minds start spinning, tallying up things that need to be done in order to get there. Such as:

- Defining use cases
- Resolving legal and privacy issues
- Picking an implementation platform
- Integrating it into our current architecture
- Securing it
- Planning for capacity
- Planning for support
- Projecting usage patterns

It is difficult for geeks to even think about something in the future if its plausibility is in question. It costs them a significant amount of effort to suspend disbelief.

Promising

Non-geeks, on the other hand, are not so sensitive about whether something is fantastical or not. They are more concerned about the future's attractiveness than its plausibility. Very often they understand questions about plausibility as objections to their imagined future. Your questions about how something might work are perceived by them as deliberate sabotage of their beautiful dreams.

How this plays out:

The judgments that arise from the Future Contraxiom are particularly insidious. You think that you are being supportive, testing their ideas to make sure that they will work when implemented. But they think that you're an annoying know-it-all who is trying to undermine them, objecting to their ideas without offering any of your own. For many non-geeks, especially the expressive ones, this is infuriating.

Inner dialogue

How non-geeks respond to the Future Contraxiom:

> "All you can talk about is what won't work."

> "You won't share in the excitement of a dream."

> "I don't even want you in the room when we are planning."

How geeks respond to the Future Contraxiom:

> "You think I'm trying to bring you down whenever I try to help."

> "Your optimism means I'm stuck managing all the risks."

"I'm afraid of your dream, because you will blame me if it's impossible."

OVERHEARD

One Bay Area app development entrepreneur said, "I come from a programming background, so normally I'm perfectly in sync with the tech people I manage. But when I found myself as the guy who had to come up with new product development ideas, I found I was very frustrated with my CTO, who seemed to be shooting every idea I had down. I had heard clients complain about their technologists before, but when I experienced it myself, I finally realized how frustrating it can be. It actually took us quite a while to work through it."

What to do

As a geek leader, you can organize how you interact with non-geek stakeholders to minimize the effects of this contraxiom.

- Plan time for focusing on the plausibility of the proposition, but refrain from considering it until you reach the scheduled time.

- Reserve time for reviewing risks and obstacles to the proposition, but don't try to do it in the same sitting.

- Write down questions and concerns as you think of them rather than blurting them out. Don't voice them until your non-geek partners are ready to hear them.

- Before shifting gears, make sure you let your partners know that you understand what is important about their proposition. If they feel that you "get it," they will more likely hear your questions and concerns in the supportive light that you intend them, rather than as objections.

* Invest time in explaining what the risks are and what they mean, framing them in terms of what is most important to your stakeholder about the proposition.

KNOWING

We come to know what we know very differently.

Geeks know in their head, through detailed analysis.

Non-geeks know in their gut, by getting the gist.

To illuminate this distinction, we're going to overemphasize the general preferences among geeks and non-geeks and treat them as if each falls into completely separate and distinct categories: analytical knowing and getting-the-gist knowing. Although in the real world the conflicting styles are not as stark, the results are still dramatic and destructive. It leads us to:

* Condescend to each other
* Dismiss valuable contributions
* Struggle for consensus

Let's look at it in more, er … detail.

Detailed analysis

Geeks know something to be true only after they have subjected it to an analytical process. They take an idea and:

* Break it down to its component parts
* Test each part for validity and, if each passes,

- Recombine them into a whole idea and test the whole for plausibility

If an idea survives this rigorous deconstruction, testing, and reconstruction process, then geeks know that it must be true. Analysis is a process driven by details. For geeks, details reveal truth.

Getting the gist

Non-geeks know something to be true when they can relate to it. They verify the truth of something by

- Viscerally connecting it to their own personal experiences
- Checking in with others to see if they agree that it is true

So non-geeks know something to be true when they can feel the meaning of the facts – good, bad, exciting, worrisome, outrageous, or gratifying. Truth is an experience; it is felt individually and reaffirmed collectively. This process is driven by feelings and can be derailed by too many details. For non-geeks, details cloud truth.

How this plays out

These opposing ways of knowing – driven by details and getting gist – prevent us from feeling as if we are on the same page. It explains why we get so frustrated trying to explain things to each other.

Geeks need details. So when they see their non-geek colleagues confused by something that they are trying to tell them, they give them exactly what they would want were they the ones who were confused: more details. Unfortunately, that's exactly the opposite of what would help the non-geeks. Heaping more details on their already clouded experience only makes things worse. At that moment, what they need is an anecdote, an example that helps them relate to all the facts.

Meanwhile, non-geeks vainly try to get geeks to get the gist of what they are saying by piling on more examples and stories, none of which really helps geeks to accept what is said as true.

When we disagree about what is true and how we should arrive at truth, our responses are intense and judgmental. When someone can't grasp the facts you consider obvious, it feels bad on both sides. It is confusing, isolating, and disturbing. The typical response is to simply dismiss the person as an idiot and ignore everything he or she says in the future. Not productive.

Inner dialogue

How non-geeks respond to the Knowing Contraxiom:

> "Your details confuse and annoy me when I need to get the big picture."

> "You infect every meeting you attend with analysis paralysis; we just need to decide already!"

> "Your condescending attachment to being right interferes with our getting results."

How geeks respond to the Knowing Contraxiom:

> "I'm offended by your attachment to being ignorant."

> "You insult me by expecting me to act based on your ever-shifting gut feelings."

> "You endanger us all with your intellectual laziness."

What to do

Geeks seeking to overcome the misunderstandings and bad feelings that arise from the Knowing Contraxiom should:

Have compassion for non-geeks' struggle to understand. Remember, when people are struggling to understand something, their confusion is not an attempt to willfully thwart or annoy you. It's not personal. In fact, they're not having a good time either.

Present information in ways that support their way of knowing rather than yours. When non-geeks aren't getting something, don't add details. Instead, use anecdotes, stories, and analogies to help them relate to the information.

Recognize that their intuition often contains valuable insights based on personal experience. Avoid the trap of overlooking the value of information arrived at in ways different from yours. You don't have to blindly accept the validity of non-geeks' intuition without putting it through your own analysis, but you should respect their intuition enough to evaluate it. You might be surprised how much wisdom their intuition can yield.

LANGUAGE

We have very different ideas about the purpose of language.

For geeks, language is for transmitting information.

For non-geeks, language is for sharing meaning.

One of the common myths about the problematic relationship between geeks and non-geeks is that the problems stem from simply not speaking each other's language, that we use different words and confuse each other. While there is some truth to this, we found that the differences over language run much deeper.

This contraxiom is about our different assumptions about what language should be used for.

When we use language for different purposes, no matter what we say, or what words we choose, we still end up with the feeling that the others just don't get it. Perhaps more than any other difference, the Language Contraxiom gives rise to a sense that we really are from different tribes and that our very sincere attempts to reach out and communicate are doomed.

But when you become aware of this contraxiom, you will be better able to overcome communication problems as they occur.

Transmitting information

For geeks, the purpose of language is to transmit information. Geeks think of language as a protocol for taking an idea from their own minds, encoding it, transmitting it to others, and having them receive those ideas, reproduced in their minds in an identical form.

In short, words and sentences are like things: concrete, literal, and breakable. An ambiguous word is a broken word. Just as imprecise code will lead to technical failure, geeks believe, vague language must be fixed. Like code, misused words or fuzzy statements must be debugged. In fact, debugging language by asking for or offering more precise definitions is great fun for geeks.

This model of language usage explains some aspects of geek behavior that non-geeks often find annoying. Geeks frequently:

* Take things very literally

- Interrupt the flow of conversation to ask clarifying questions
- Correct what other people say
- Send highly detailed, formal emails

It is another example of taking what works well for creating technology and applying it, with limited success, to human relationships. It works fine when you are relating to someone who shares your assumptions about the purpose of language, but it breaks down when trying to communicate with people who hold a different worldview about language use.

Sharing meaning

Non-geeks tend to use language to share meaning, which is very different from transmitting data. Sharing meaning is less about moving information from one place to another and more about triggering a shared inner state between the speaker and the listener. Non-geeks' goal is to create a shared subjective experience of the facts, more so than to matter of factly describe the world.

There may be some overlap here, since for geeks, an elegantly stated description of the world creates a resoundingly positive experience, but in general, geeks care very little about how you feel as you are evaluating the information. In contrast, non-geeks care very much that the feeling triggered by the facts are shared. In a work setting, those feelings might include importance, surprise, excitement, satisfaction, worry, outrage, and urgency.

So non-geeks tend to be much less rigorous about word choice and factual accuracy in everyday conversation. For them, vague word choices don't need to be fixed. Minor inconsistencies don't need to be debugged.

The Language Contraxiom is especially evident when you consider poetry. In our workshops, we ask the geeks in the room whether or not they like poetry, and when Paul declares that he hates it, there is ample agreement. Then Maria describes how thrilling it is when the exact right word appears in the exact right place in a poem, and the meaning of that word, instead of being limited and literal, explodes with multiple ambiguous and evocative meanings, creating a feeling of awe. The non-geek crowd tends to nod in agreement.

How this plays out

This difference means we don't naturally make great music together. What geeks consider to be helpful and worthy, such as offering more meticulous definitions or asking exceedingly precise questions, non-geeks often find condescending, nit-picky, and petty. What non-geeks consider to be rousing and galvanizing, geeks often find fuzzy, ineffectual, and superfluous.

In short, we miss each other's cues. Non-geeks need to feel that their co-workers share an emotional drive that unites them as a team. Geeks need to agree on facts and measures of success. The result is that everyone questions one another's commitment to the success of their joint enterprise, sapping enthusiasm and provoking resentment.

Inner dialogue

How non-geeks respond to the Language Contraxiom:

"You are annoyingly literal."

"You interrupt the flow of conversation with picky little questions."

"You make it way too hard to talk to you."

How geeks respond to the Language Contraxiom:

"You are so vague I can't figure out what you are talking about."

"You get annoyed when I try to clarify your statements."

"You take the fun out of clarifying things."

What to do

As a geek leader, there's not much you can do to change how your team or your colleagues use language. But you can be aware of the difference and exemplify forbearance. Here are some ideas:

Explicitly point out what you consider important to the project. You don't need to emote inauthentically. Just say what matters to you.

Practice patience and tolerance for ambiguity. Before trying to help your communication partner to be more precise, pause to consider whether or not the content of what he is talking about even needs precision at this time.

Offer non-geeks the satisfaction of sharing their meaning, or at least recognizing what is important to them.

When summarizing facts, describe the implications in terms that will help non-geeks get the meaning. "This is exciting because …" or "This might concern you because …"

LYING

We profoundly disagree about the definition and significance of lying.

> For geeks, lying is evil.

> For non-geeks, lying is impolite.

The Lying Contraxiom is perhaps the most fun because it is immediately recognizable, while hiding in plain sight. For many geeks, it is startling that something so true would have remained unarticulated for so long. For non-geeks, it is shocking to find out that seemingly innocuous behavior could be perceived as vile.

Evil

For geeks, lying is evil. It's not just a little bit bad; it's *really* bad. It is a sin against Truth, which for geeks is a sacred thing. To lie is to deny the very thing that holds geeks together as a tribe, their common recognition of objectively verifiable truth.

Perhaps even more importantly, geeks have a different definition than non-geeks of what constitutes a lie. For geeks, you're lying if you say something you don't absolutely know to be true.

To geeks, some common figures of speech like exaggerations, hyperbole, and opinions stated as fact are lies, and as such can be deeply offensive.

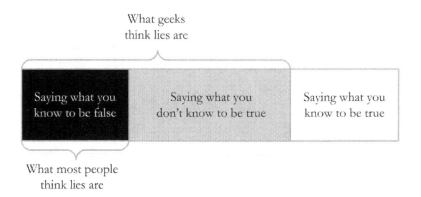

Impolite

For non-geeks, lying is more like bad manners. Sure, their mothers told them that lying was wrong, and they don't necessarily like to do it. But they have no qualms about stretching the truth to achieve a goal or spare someone's feelings. Little white lies are not cataclysmic sins against nature. In fact, sometimes they are just the social lubricant required to allow people to get along.

And non-geeks define lying much more loosely than geeks. For non-geeks, you're only lying if you say something you absolutely know to be false.

To non-geeks, you're not lying if you use exaggeration, hyperbole, or opinions – these are normal, acceptable ways of expressing enthusiasm, magnitude, or perspective.

How this plays out

What's particularly unusual about the Lying Contraxiom is that it elicits an emotional response from geeks rather than from non-geeks. Because lying is a violation of geeks' deep reverence for truth, and because geeks are so rarely seen as volatile, the speed and force of the reaction often comes as a shock to non-geeks, who normally think of their colleagues as emotionless and robotic.

Another aspect of the Lying Contraxiom is that it fuels one of the most common examples of geek/non-geek conflict. It can be very difficult to get estimates from technical people about when things will be done. Non-geeks almost always assume that geeks refuse to provide this because they don't want to be held accountable. But very often geeks refuse to answer these questions because they don't want to lie. To give an estimate is to say something you don't know absolutely to be true, and therefore it is to tell a lie, something geeks find deeply painful.

When you explain this to non-geeks, you can almost see years of pent-up frustration and anger draining from their faces. They suddenly realize that what they considered self-centered, destructive behavior is in fact a principled and moral stand – even if it can be dysfunctional and difficult.

Inner dialogue

How geeks respond to the Lying Contraxiom:

"You baffle me by asking me to lie to you."

"You violate me with your hyperbole and exaggerations."

"Your flippant disregard of Truth makes this an unsafe place to work."

How non-geeks respond to the Lying Contraxiom:

"Your reticence holds us back."

"You qualify everything you say and everything I say. It drives me crazy."

"You get so upset over the strangest things."

AN EXAMPLE FROM THE EXTREME

The insight for the Lying Contraxiom came from reading about autism, not because we believe that geeks are autistic, but because we were interested in understanding the fairly well-documented prevalence of Asperger's syndrome among engineers. We found a fascinating account of an informal experiment done by a Rhode Island social skills teacher in the book *The Unwritten Rules of Social Relationships*, by Temple Grandin and Sean Barron. After observing that many of her autistic students became surprisingly stressed when asked to lie, she decided to have a conversation about it with two of her classes of teenage boys.

The first class was a group of non-autistic boys. She asked them to talk about lying, and almost right away they became animated and self-organizing. A lively, nuanced discussion ensued in which the boys named various types of lies, when it was okay to lie (to parents to get out of trouble, for example) and when it wasn't (about drug use). The teacher said "They *loved* the exercise and were animated in describing how they can tell if someone is lying by their tone of voice, eye contact, posture, etc."

Then, in a classroom of autistic boys, she introduced the same topic and received a very different response. The boys were adamant that they didn't lie. They had hard and fast rules for themselves, saying, "You should never lie" and "You should tell the truth." In their minds, these rules were absolute, and there was no nuance to the question. When probed about the concept of white lies, several of them said, "I'm confused." They had trouble accepting the fact that other people lie or that it would ever be an acceptable option, and had trouble detecting when other people were lying to them.

"What was most startling was the emotional toll just talking about the subject of honesty and lying had taken on the autism spectrum boys." Two of the boys broke down into tears when they each recounted a story of having lied years before. "He related that, in the first grade (remember, these kids are teenagers now), students would get stickers for reading books. He hated to read books, so he would say he read them when he had not. No sooner did the words leave his mouth then he put his head down and began to wail."

Shortly after that, the students said they had had enough, and one "insisted that lying would never, ever be talked about in group again."

Said the teacher, "This is one of the few times we have experienced such strong, anxiety-ridden, emotional reactions from students in our social skills group when discussing any topic."

What to do

Because geeks are the ones who react so strongly to this contraxiom, wouldn't it be nice if the non-geeks would recognize their sensitivities and just not lie? Until that happens, it's important for geeks to realize that their strong reactions to lies and judgments about liars are a problem for them. There are several things geeks can do to minimize the effect of this attitude on the relationship.

- *Resist the urge to qualify sweeping statements.* Non-geeks don't consider overgeneralization a problem. It's best to evaluate whether it's important to perfect their language in a particular situation rather than reflexively adding precision when it's not required. Every time a geek interrupts a non-geek, it's one more small annoyance that leads them to resist clarification when it is really important.

- *Recognize non-geeks' hyperbole as descriptive, not literal.* Non-geeks often use hyperbole as a way of emphasizing a point, not as a deliberate attempt to oversimplify or mislead. Think carefully before interrupting them, since it is particularly distressing to them to be interrupted when they are in the throes of enthusiasm, which is when they're most likely to use hyperbole in the first place. Don't quash their enthusiasm with excessive precision.

- *Clarify the difference between targets, estimates, and promises.* As much as geeks hate to lie about the future, and often fear that even the wildest guess will be construed as a promise, they do need to recognize that non-geeks need information about timing in order to plan and coordinate their activities with them. Clarify exactly what you mean when giving an estimate and confirm that they have heard whether you're giving them a target, an estimate, or a promise.

OVERHEARD

As the business owner of an app development project, my cross-functional team and I were huddled around the project manager's desk, reviewing a presentation we were about to give to the executive team. It was all cool until we got to a slide that had a date on it. Brad, the tech lead, said in a low, menacing voice, "Get that date out of there." The project manager and I looked at each other. She was a non-geek like me, and we were both wondering, "What has gotten into Brad?" Normally, he is so chill, so together, easy-going, and kind. What's with this terrifying edge in his voice? And in the time it took for us to exchange glances, Brad's face had gotten beet-red, he was breathing through clenched teeth, and he said even more forcefully, "Take it out." So the project manager scrambled to hit the delete button, and then Brad calmed down. Only later, after learning about contraxioms, did I realize that he was so upset because he didn't want to lie.

GOOD

We see good and evil with different degrees of absolutism.

For geeks, good is absolute.

For non-geeks, good is contextual.

The Good Contraxiom is, at its heart, about inflexibility, the harsh judgment that stems from it, and the difficulties that creates when we try to work together. It is perhaps the toughest pill for many geeks to swallow.

Geeks tend toward black-and-white thinking. It is, in part, what draws them to technical work in the first place. For them, there's something comforting about working with systems that they can expect to respond predictably. When you run the same piece of code, under the same conditions, you always get the same answer.

So it's not surprising that geeks expect the people they work with to adhere to principles to the same degree. Here, as in some of the other contraxioms, geeks apply a standard to a domain where it may not be entirely appropriate.

The tendency toward black-and-white thinking is by no means limited to geeks, but we find that it shows up distinctly in work settings when geeks and non-geeks try to work together. Geeks hold tight to principles that they apply rather inflexibly, while non-geeks unwittingly violate these principles willy-nilly, causing geeks to form harsh judgments about the characters of these violators. When this happens, geeks get a reputation for being stubborn, condescending jerks who no one wants to work with. Non-geeks, in their attempts to deflect this unpleasantness, fall into a type of retaliatory judgment that often looks egregious and unfair, because non-geeks, more expressive and emotional, can sometimes be flamboyantly open about how they feel.

This leads to a self-perpetuating cycle of harsh judgment and mutual mistrust. While geeks often suffer greatly by being judged and sidelined in their organizations, in our analysis, this particular cycle usually starts with geeks because they expect non-geeks to conform to their more rigid standards of principled behavior.

Geek leaders who want to be successful must be on the lookout for this contraxiom and the tendency toward judgment when it arises. To avoid having you and your team sidelined, you need to set an example of forbearance, acceptance, and thinking that is flexible enough to support productive collaboration.

Absolute

Geeks, as consummate abstract thinkers, have a tendency to see values in black-and-white terms. If something is good, it is always good, at all times, in all settings. If something is bad, it is always bad, at all times, in all settings. Rules and principles are what make life livable. If unchanging rules and constraints are essential for problem-solving in the mathematical and technological realms, doesn't it follow that they should be similarly rigid in the social realm? Here are some examples of principles that geeks hold sacrosanct that are frequently unwittingly transgressed at work:

Fairness. People should be rewarded based on the value they produce. "He got sent to two conferences this year, while I wasn't allowed to go to even one. I wrote twice as much code as he did. This place is so unfair!"

Consistency. People are supposed to know what they want and not change their minds. "On Tuesday she wanted the report sorted by date; now she wants it sorted by customer last name. And she doesn't even have the decency to apologize."

Honesty. People should speak the truth at all times. "We worked all weekend because he said it needed to launch on

Monday. It's Monday and he isn't even ready with his stuff. He was lying about how urgent it was just to manipulate us."

Process. People should follow the processes that have been established. "She calls Shawn directly rather than getting in queue at the help desk like everyone else. We've told her three times that requests need to be prioritized and assigned by the help desk manager. She thinks the rules don't apply to her."

Essentially, when geeks see people break the rules, renege on agreements, or bend the truth, many of them will have extremely visceral, negative responses. The rules are there to help delineate good from bad, and breaking rules is bad, so people who break rules are bad.

For geeks, such unprincipled people can't be trusted, since adherence to principles is the primary factor in assessing whether or not someone is trustworthy. This criterion for trust is very, very different for many non-geeks, which we shall see in our next contraxiom. And it runs deep, touches many emotional chords, and leads to numerous relationship breakdowns.

In short, to geeks, if you do bad things, you are a bad person.

Contextual

Non-geeks are generally not as attached to rules and principles as geeks are, at least not about the same kinds of things. Non-geeks can be just as unbending about their political or religious beliefs, but they are less likely to be morally outraged when the software development process is not rigorously adhered to. And they are more likely to stretch the truth when describing capabilities to clients. Nor would they think it's a problem to change their minds. And their sense of fairness might be less exquisitely tuned.

This isn't because they are unprincipled; it is because rules and principles play a much less significant role in their work lives. They are more likely to go with the flow, feel out a situation, and respond to a scenario based on instincts born from experience. Intuition works well for them, and they see no need to codify their sense of good and bad in a rigid set of rules.

There are numerous examples of truly amoral people, but we suggest that there are also many instances of kind-hearted, hard-working, well-meaning people who get classified by geeks as evil because they violated rules they didn't even know existed.

Non-geek morality has a lot more shades of gray in it, and a lot more qualifications. Sometimes ends are important enough to compromise principles. Non-geeks believe that, sometimes, good people do bad things.

How this plays out

The Good Contraxiom leads to some of the ugliest frustrations of all. Since geeks tend toward black-and-white thinking about good and bad and believe that people who do bad things are bad people, it's easy for them to fall into the trap of judging others quickly and harshly. This is how they get the reputation of being dismissive and condescending. It's also how they alienate others, convincing people that they are not "on their side."

These judgments are different from the ones that arise from the Knowing Contraxiom, which tends to lead to judgments about intelligence. The Good Contraxiom often leads to more cutting judgments of character. Black-and-white thinking also leads to inflexibility when responding to new challenges and unforeseen events.

Inner dialogue

How geeks respond to the Good Contraxiom:

> "You act like the rules don't apply to you."

> "You have no morals."

How non-geeks respond to the Good Contraxiom:

> "You hide behind rigid rules so you won't be held accountable for results."

> "Your inflexibility is maddening."

> "Who are you to judge me?"

What to do

To avoid the traps of inflexibility and harsh judgment, geeks need to do three things:

Recognize when you've fallen into the trap. The best way to do this is to notice your own sense of outrage, because for geeks, this sort of anger at work is rarely triggered by anything other than a perceived violation of principles. Without a conscious recognition that you are reacting to this contraxiom, there's little you can do to avoid an escalating cycle of judgment and mistrust.

Question whether a real violation has occurred. Often, you may discover that:

* Non-geeks may be applying conflicting and perhaps more important principles.

* There may be good reasons for the current situation to qualify as an exception to the rule.

- The principle that you are presuming a non-geek violated may not be worthy of being a principle at all.

Discuss your concerns with your colleagues respectfully, exposing the principles you consider important. You might say:

"Let me see if I understand. You want to skip testing so we can get the functionality in time for the trade show. It seems as if you are prioritizing speed-to-market over user experience. Does that sound right? I have to say, it goes against my principles to release products that cause users to experience bugs. My team and I place high value on error-free technology, and it will be demoralizing to the team to ask them to release something that has a very high likelihood of breaking."

By respectfully exposing the principles that are being violated, you are giving your colleagues a chance to recognize what is at stake for you and possibly to adjust their positions. At least you are giving them a chance to appreciate the emotional toll it might take on the tech team.

Truly unscrupulous people will not respond well, but most well-meaning colleagues will willingly engage in a discussion about the principles at stake.

WANTING

Geeks and non-geeks value desire and its role in decision-making very differently.

For geeks, wanting should be irrelevant to decision-making.

For non-geeks, wanting is essential for decision-making.

The Wanting Contraxiom is about what we consider an appropriate role for the feeling of desire in the workplace.

Irrelevant

Geeks believe that decisions in the workplace should be based exclusively on facts and logic. They mistrust decisions that are based on what someone wants or doesn't want, because they see desire as fleeting, arbitrary, and changeable. They prefer to arrive at decisions through an analytical process, designed to identify the option that is best for the organization. In fact, the analytical process itself is specifically designed to eliminate emotion as a criterion in decision-making.

Geeks also feel that when people in the workplace ask something just because they want it, they are being selfish and immature, like a child who wants a pony for his birthday. We almost instinctively see such people as petulant children, stomping their feet and demanding their desires be met.

For example, you might want to convince your boss to replace several old servers. You would be unlikely to march into your boss's office and say, "I hate these three servers and want to replace them." You would be much more likely to go in with a well-prepared list of reasons justifying the cost of replacement, a list that would never include your personal annoyance with the inconveniences of old technology.

The irony is that, while non-geeks are interested in the reasons, many of them are more persuaded, more galvanized, and more likely to be moved to action by the seemingly selfish statement of what you want.

Essential

We're not suggesting that non-geeks ignore facts in their decision-making processes. For some decisions, they consider analysis to be just as essential as geeks do. But they also consider subjective criteria in addition to purely rational ones. In fact, non-geeks feel quite uncomfortable making a decision without a strong feeling that it is right.

What's more, when you are asking non-geeks to make decisions based solely on factual and logical information that you've provided them, they're unlikely to trust you or your information, for two very good reasons.

- They assume that all people have desires, and if you are asking for something without exposing yours, then you must be concealing them deliberately. If you are hiding what you want, you must have some ulterior motive in asking for it.

- People with wants are more predictable than people with nothing but information. If decisions are made solely on the basis of information, you may need to re-examine the decisions constantly as you learn new things.

And for non-geeks, wanting isn't stained by the presumption of selfishness. It represents the synthesis of reason. When they hear, "I want to upgrade the servers because I'm sick of the hassle," they fill in the gaps, imagining that the hassles must be very great indeed to make you want the servers gone. The fact of your emotional response to the situation is important information to them. It gives them:

- A synthesized summary of the importance of the situation

- A sense of your commitment to the solution and its urgency

- An opportunity to adjust their desires in response – in relationship – to yours.

This is the key element. What someone wants, relative to what you want, is a key factor for building relationships. And while geeks might feel secure about relationships where all parties agree on the facts, non-geeks feel more secure about relationships where all parties have aligned their desires.

When you deprive non-geeks access to your desires, you deprive them of the opportunity to truly relate to you, as a person, with a subjective reality.

In short, non-geeks can never really trust people without wants. To them, they seem uncommitted, apathetic, and unreliable.

How this plays out

Non-geeks are frustrated by what seems to them to be geek apathy. They are looking for emotional cues of commitment and urgency, only to find dispassionate reason. What geeks consider to be evidence of their commitment doesn't register as such with non-geeks. "How could you think that I'm not committed? I was here all weekend wasn't I?" So geeks feel frustrated and underappreciated, while non-geeks feel suspicious.

Inner dialogue

How geeks respond to the Wanting Contraxiom:

"I gave you all these facts, so why don't you come to the right conclusion?"

"You act like what you want is more important than what's right."

"You won't be swayed by reason."

How non-geeks respond to the Wanting Contraxiom:

"You sit in judgment of decisions you aren't willing to make."

"You don't seem to really care about anything. You've got no sense of urgency."

"Your aloofness makes it seem as if you're not on my team."

What to do

The good news is that the solution to the problem is relatively simple for geek leaders to implement.

Simply start saying things that express what you want. There are lots of ways of indicating that you desire a specific outcome. The real hurdle is to become comfortable expressing your own desire. It might make it easier if you begin to think of expressing desire not as a purely emotional thing.

An expression of desire is a summary of what is important to you.

Take the example of requesting permission to upgrade those old, annoying servers. In addition to stating the reasons for doing so, add something like, "Honestly, I'm really tired of wasting so much time on these problem machines and really want to focus on more important things. "

Notice that you can express a personal want without it being at all selfish; that you don't need to use florid, emotional language; and that you can include what you want as a fact relevant to the situation.

Here are a few ideas for how you can comfortably express your desire:

- "I really want the users to love this new interface."

- "I'm committed to making that deadline."

- "I'm excited by the prospect of getting this fixed."

CONCLUSION: CONTRAXIOM SPOTTING

If you have arrived at the end of this chapter, you are probably a curious sort. Perhaps each contraxiom had a ring of truth for you. Perhaps you have experienced the sting of outrage at observations made with scant evidence. In either case, you probably wonder, "And now that I see more deeply into worldview differences, what am I supposed to do with this knowledge?" That is what the rest of the book explores. We will look in detail at specific, real-world implications for leading geeks.

But there is another way to use this information. Now that you know that contrasting worldviews underlie many conflicts, you can use this exercise as a springboard for practicing a new skill: contraxiom spotting.

As a contraxiom spotter, you will follow this simple process:

1. Notice and try to name the axiomatic belief that fuels expressed opinions.

2. Notice your own sense of the rightness or wrongness of the axiom, and suspend it for a moment.

3. Imagine the purpose that the axiom serves in that person's life, such as:

   - Providing a feeling of safety.

   - Supporting a feeling of mastery, by organizing thoughts and actions.

   - Giving a sense of belonging with other people who share that belief.

4. Allow yourself three seconds of empathy for the human being who lives with that axiom.

5. Continue your interaction, adjusting your approach, your tone, or your objectives based on your empathetic insight.

The rewards of noticing contraxioms and adjusting to them are immense.

- It restores the humanity to the people you disagree with.

- It allows you to face them with budding compassion, rather than piercing contempt.

- It fosters a collaborative relationship for both of you, rather than a combative one.

- It creates just enough space for something new, unforeseen, and mutually beneficial to happen.

Contraxiom spotting can be done anywhere, anytime. Use it at home with your spouse or your teen. Use it with your brother-in-law at the next barbecue. Use it with colleagues at work. Use it during project post-mortems when feelings run high. Use it with the people on your teams who are much, much geekier than you.

While it's possible that this approach to discord is new to you, you might recognize it as a variation of advice dating back thousands of years. And you will be correct. Empathy is a tried-and-true way for human beings to resolve conflict and promote collaboration, and these contraxioms are offered as a reasoned approach to encouraging empathy in the workplace and in our lives.

We, the authors, have been living with contraxioms for over four years now, and this model has been profoundly beneficial. This book would not have been possible if we didn't have contraxiom spotting as a tool. The awareness of a contraxiom at play didn't dissolve our disagreements about work, but it created the space – a richly empathetic space – for us to be creative about resolving discord. The result is that we have created something that we believe to be useful to people who are in situations similar to ours, and that seems rather rare. We don't know of any geeks or non-geeks who have willingly allowed their worldviews to clash often and painfully enough to learn these lessons and write them down. We share this because we don't expect contraxiom spotting to be easy for you, but we do predict that it will be richly rewarding.

PART II

MANAGING YOURSELF AND OTHERS

ADVANCE YOUR CAREER IN ONE SIMPLE STEP

We wrote this chapter as a response to the maddening array of impractical and excessively complex career advice that has been foisted on geeks for decades. We have been pleasantly surprised by the kind reception this powerful but simple approach has received as we have presented it to audiences on three continents. Written in Paul's voice, it draws heavily from his personal experience.

You don't need another list of 24 things you can do to advance your career this year. No one has time to focus on that many things, and honestly most of them make little difference. It's better to select one thing that will make a big difference and focus on that exclusively. So this year, I suggest you advance your career by doing only one thing. There's probably no single investment in your career that will pay off more.

Think less about yourself and more about the people around you.

Don't worry. I'm not suggesting that the world will be filled with flowers and puppies if we all stop being selfish and self-centered. I'm not talking about trying to change the fundamentals of human nature. This is a pragmatic and reasoned approach for geeks to respond to changes in the technical labor market.

To grasp why focusing on other people's experience is the best thing you can do for your career, let's get started by examining the changing context of technical jobs.

THE FUTURE OF GEEK CAREERS

We're all contractors now

For nearly 30 years, the nature of employment has been rapidly evolving. The idea of working your whole career for a single company is long dead. More and more people are becoming contractors, mobile and independent. In fact, one recent study predicted that by 2020 half of the American workforce will be independent contractors. And even for the people who have traditional jobs, stability will remain elusive.

This isn't necessarily something to be upset about. Chances are that no one is slamming doors in your face, preventing you from pursuing your dreams. But neither is anyone waiting to open doors for you.

If you want a great career, you're going to have to create it for yourself. No matter how fantastic your company or nurturing your boss, their primary role is not to plan the trajectory of your career. Whether you get the chance to have a fulfilling and lucrative work life is up to you. Even if you're not a contractor, you need to start thinking like one.

Mainstream advice is inadequate

Most career advice is aimed at people with very different worldviews than us geeks. Few of us chase power, money, or fame. We'd die of boredom with a four-hour workweek. And we don't look to our careers to provide spiritual enlightenment.

To us, the quality of our career is measured by the nature of the problems we get to solve, the elegance of the solutions we get to build, and the difference we make with those solutions. For us, career planning is about figuring out how to get the chance to solve great problems on an ongoing basis.

Mainstream career advice rarely takes this into account. So you end up wading through suggestions that just don't seem to apply. Most of the latest ideas seem to cluster into three distinct themes.

Unhelpful Suggestion #1: Follow your passion

Do you have a mission statement for your career? Do you really know where you want to be 15 years from now? Ten? Five? Next year? Yeah. I didn't think so.

It's unrealistic. In technology, things change too fast. No one really knows what technology will be important or even how IT jobs will be structured 10 years from now. Will we all be contractors? Will computers start programming themselves? Will the cloud eliminate the need for internal IT departments? (Okay, I doubt that any of these will happen, but they have all been predicted.)

Passion is not our way. We pride ourselves on being a rather dispassionate lot, devoted to logic.

Unhelpful Suggestion #2: Develop your skills

This is unhelpful because we'd prefer to do this and nothing else. We geeks are very comfortable with the idea of developing our skills. We love learning new technologies, piling up credentials, and playing different project roles. When geeks talk about career development, we focus almost exclusively on skill development.

Unfortunately, skill growth doesn't necessarily lead to career development. We just like to think it will because we love learning. It's true that you might not get a job because of a lack of skills, but it doesn't follow that having skills creates job opportunities. The highway of technology career advancement is littered with rusting heaps that used to be highly skilled, fine-tuned machines but stalled because someone forgot to put gas in the tank. As we will see, the real fuel for your career is not a new set of wheels; it is the good will you generate by being good to work with.

So while developing skills is good advice for the general population, for us it's like giving heroin to an addict. Adding one more certification to your résumé will make little difference in your ability to get the opportunity to work with good people on meaty problems.

Unhelpful Suggestion #3: Grow your network

Of all the common advice, this one may be the most inappropriate for us.

We tend to be introverts. The idea of attending events with dozens or hundreds or thousands of people that I don't know and have no reason to meet other than a vague sense that they might be helpful in the future sounds like torture to me. Even the less mercenary version of seeking to meet random people with the intention of being helpful to them gives me the horrors.

We might be slightly more comfortable with the idea of virtual networking in social media. This can be a good tool for maintaining existing relationships, but it's no substitute for genuine human connection.

How Focusing on Others Advances Your Career

A new model, just for geeks

What we need is a way to think about career development that is compatible with both our personalities and the nature of the work we do. We need to think about what a successful career looks like in light of unpredictable technological change and high labor mobility. So if we assume that chaos is the norm, then long-range planning, devising an artificially stable goal, is a waste of time. We need to think about this in more probabilistic terms.

In (pseudo) mathematical terms, it might look something like this:

Probability (Fulfilling Career) =

f (Number of Opportunities,
Ability to Select Wisely)

Where:

Number of Opportunities = How many job/project opportunities you are aware of and are offered

Ability to Select Wisely = Your ability to select from among the options in ways that maximize your career fulfillment

In other words, the more opportunities you have and the more able you are to select from them in ways you find fulfilling, the more likely you are to have a fulfilling career.

I'm not going to presume to tell you what your criteria for selecting opportunities should be. That's up to you. But no matter what your personal preferences are, the more opportunities you have to choose from, the more likely you are to have some good options. So if we agree that the key variable to focus on is generating opportunities, the question is "How?"

How geeks can generate opportunities

This is where we as geeks have to confront a rather disturbing truth. We assume that the number of opportunities presented to us should be based solely on the degree of our skills. We presume that if life were fair, the smartest and most productive people would always be in the highest demand. That's why we invest so heavily in skill development. The reality is something like this:

Number of Opportunities =

f (Luck, Capabilities) + f (Capabilities, Quality of Experience, Top of Mind Awareness)

Where:

Luck = The random chance that you find an opportunity through no intentional effort of your own or of anyone you know

Capabilities = The breadth and depth of your technical, organizational, and managerial skills

Quality of Experience = How positively people feel about their experience working with you

Top of Mind Awareness = How likely people who know you are to think of you when they become aware of an opportunity

In other words, there are two basic ways opportunities arrive on your doorstep in this environment. In both cases, your capabilities are not the dominant factor in drawing opportunities toward you.

Scenario 1: Pure luck

You get lucky, and fantastic opportunities magically rain down upon you that fit perfectly with your skill set. This is nice when it happens, but you might not want to bet your career on it being a regular occurrence. You can't really control this.

Scenario 2: Good experience

This one you have a lot more control over. The people who know you bring opportunities to you that they think would be a good fit for you. As people move from job to job or contract to contract, they find problems that need solving and positions that need to be filled. So who do they call? They call the people they feel comfortable with and confident about. They call people who they feel are:

- Competent

- Trustworthy

- Good to work with

- Someone they are proud to refer

- And someone that comes to mind as a good fit for the problem they're trying to solve

In short, people bring opportunities to people that they have had a good experience working with in the past.

Now you see how you can advance your career in one simple step. The more you pay attention to the experience that the people around you have of working with you, the more likely they are in the future to invite you to do more work. Paying more attention to their experience is not only a nice thing to do that makes you more effective in your current position; it is also an investment in your future career prospects.

Paul's story of Eduardo and Tom

A few years back I worked with a man named Eduardo who didn't seem to be following any of the career advice you hear these days. He didn't have a mission statement. He didn't work his brand. He didn't go out for beers with us after work. He wasn't outgoing or extroverted in any way. But I would jump at the chance to work with him again, and I would be happy to refer him to any of the people in my network, confident that he would do a good job for them and make me look good in their eyes.

On another project, I worked with a very affable man named Tom. He was smart, friendly, outgoing, and full of ideas. He socialized with everyone and always wanted to help. But I would not choose to work with him again and probably wouldn't recommend him for much of anything.

The difference is that Eduardo, in his own introverted way, was very focused on more than just doing his job well. He was also very attentive to how the rest of us were experiencing working with him. He paid attention to some very basic things that made working with him a great experience. Here's what he did:

- When he communicated, he made sure we understood.

- When he said he'd do something, he did it or kept us informed on his progress.

- When he saw someone struggling with the workload, he offered to pitch in.

- When he made a mistake, he took responsibility for the error and the impact it had on others.

- When he saw opportunities to streamline our work, he respectfully brought them to our attention.

- When he worked with other people, not just his boss, he was consistently thoughtful and helpful.

In short, he was trustworthy. Based on my experience of working with him, I trust his work ethic, his values, and his competence.

Tom had a different approach. While he was friendly, he didn't put much effort into giving other people a good experience of him as a work partner. He was highly skilled in a narrow range of processes. He made sure that we knew that he knew the right way to do things. He was rigid and didn't listen to other people's points of view. In the end, he got little done. Based on my experience of working with him, I couldn't in good conscience recommend him to anyone else. I'm not confident that he'd do a good job, but I am pretty sure that he would make me look bad for having recommended him. However, I'd gladly go out to dinner with him, because he's a very nice guy and great company.

I tell you about Eduardo and Tom because they represent two vastly different approaches to focusing on the experience that your colleagues and customers have of you. If you follow most of the career advice that is out there, you are more likely to end up like Tom, focusing on networking and skill building, while neglecting what is the real fuel of any career, what draws opportunities to you: the quality of the experience people have of working with you.

How you can become everyone's go-to geek

Now that you have a sense of how important it is to give people the feeling that you are good to work with, you might be a little annoyed or perplexed, saying to yourself, "I studied computer science, not psychology! How am I supposed to know how to do this?"

The good news is this represents a huge opportunity, and you don't have to be Dr. Phil to take advantage of it. Thinking just a little about other people's experience can give you a tremendous competitive advantage in the technical labor market. People who work in technology have a reputation of being incredibly difficult to work with, and if you give people the feeling that you are helpful, thoughtful, and reliable, you will shine like a road flare on a dark night.

Predictable resistance

Most geeks, when first encountering the idea of creating a good work experience for their colleagues and customers, feel vaguely resistant. We like to focus on objective reality, not subjective experience. In part, that's why we chose to work with technology in the first place. Creating a subjective experience for another person seems wrong, somehow intrusive, manipulative, and inappropriate.

You're going to just have to get over it. Creating a good experience for another person is not the same thing as self-serving manipulation.

Other people, non-geeks, don't have this aversion. In fact, they expect you to think about their experience and to work to make it a good one. Not only do they expect it, but they are appalled when we don't. They are frequently mystified by what they see as our callous disregard of their feelings, when we're just trying to respect their boundaries. But remember, your intentions are invisible to them.

So let's get down to some practical advice for giving other people a positive experience of working with you.

6 ways to create a good experience of working with you

Here are six simple things you can do to give the people you work with a good experience of you as a work colleague.

1. When you communicate, make sure you are understood.

When we give presentations, one of our favorite slides says, "Messaging is not communicating." Broadcasting is what most geeks do, and that's not the same thing at all. Too many of us think that communicating looks something like this:

* Gather data

* List it in an email

* Hit send

* Wait three weeks

* Blame the other person when he doesn't respond or follow directions

But the responsibility for making sure an important message was received and understood is on you. Here are a few things you need to do to ensure that your message gets through.

Tell them why it matters. Many people can't process information without some sense of context, urgency, or responsibility for it. Most people need to be told why they should care before they can even begin to pay attention to information.

Make it safe to ask questions. A lot of people don't like to ask us questions, because all too often we give them confusing answers that sound condescending. If they feel that asking you a question is going to result in a barrage of useless details and a feeling of inadequacy, they're not going to bother asking. Let them know that you expect them to have questions, since this is not their specialty, and that you'll be happy to answer as best you can. Then take pains to explain things in a way that they can understand.

Help them through their confusion. Sometimes people don't even know what questions to ask. They know that they are confused, but don't have enough understanding to even formulate a coherent question. This makes them feel really bad. Be on the lookout for puzzled expressions. When you notice one, just say something like, "You look confused. Can I help?" They will then try to explain what they understood, and you get the chance to make sure that they got what you wanted them to get.

If you want people to have a good experience of working with you, you need to take responsibility not only for what you say, but also for ensuring that they got the message.

2. When you say you'll do something, do it, or keep people informed on your progress.

Most geeks are extraordinarily committed to doing what they promise. Despite our rather dismal industry-wide project-delivery record, most of us deeply care about hitting deadlines. So when we find that we can't fulfill on one of our promises, it's rather painful to call up the person we've let down and tell him.

So what do we do? We avoid it. We justify it to ourselves. "Oh, John is busy and won't notice that I'm late." "I'll catch up on the weekend, and Friday is the same as Monday, right?"

What you don't realize is that as painful as missed deadlines are for your colleagues, mismanaged expectations are much, much worse. Unforeseen delays are things that people can relate to and often make allowances for. But mysterious, unexplained non-delivery makes people crazy. They invent stories to explain it, stories about you that are not flattering and will not advance your career.

You must keep people informed when you don't meet their expectations, otherwise they will think the worst of you and not want to work with you in the future.

3. When you see someone struggling, offer to pitch in.

Everyone is busy and stressed these days. But there's a difference between being busy and being overwhelmed. You can see when someone is thrashing. They are highly active, frenzied even, but nothing is getting done. It's a lot like seeing an overwhelmed computer thrash.

When you see someone in that situation, offer to help if you can. Just say something like, "I can see that you've got way too many things on your plate. Is there anything I can do to help?" Even if you can't, she will really appreciate your noticing her difficulty.

Obviously, you can't help other people at the expense of getting your own work done, but often there are things you can do with very little effort that make a big difference for them.

And if you are going above and beyond, it's wise to humbly note that you are stepping outside your normal role. Not only will it make people appreciate the effort, but it will also help avoid any future role confusion, lest they get the idea that this is what you usually do.

This also triggers the Law of Reciprocation, a concept highlighted by Robert Cialdini, in which he notes that human beings are wired to return favors. A favor freely given is one of the most powerful ways to establish relationships with other people, because their biological imperative tells them to respond in kind someday. Perhaps that day will be when their new company is looking for a new director of infrastructure, and they just happen to think of you *(Cialdini, 1984)*.

4. When you make a mistake, take responsibility for the error, the impact it had, and the resolution.

There are few things at work that cause more outrage than someone ducking responsibility for mistakes. Small problems can suddenly escalate into huge battles when people try to avoid accountability. The initial mistake is no longer the issue at hand, but when people's innate sense of justice is violated, it triggers powerful reactions.

At the same time, nothing can defuse a tense situation faster than simply acknowledging your part in creating it. To do this, all you have to do is:

- Take responsibility for the facts of what happened

- Acknowledge the impact it had on the others

- Say how you will avoid it in the future

If these three things don't happen, the stink of the mistake will stick to you. You will be remembered as someone who can't be trusted. If these three things do happen, it's very likely that you will be seen as human, be forgiven, and be considered a trusted colleague.

In fact, people usually trust those who take responsibility for their mistakes much more than people who appear to make no mistakes at all.

5. When you see something that could be improved, make appropriate suggestions.

When you see opportunities for improvement, you have three options:

- Complain (either privately or publicly)

- Do nothing, because it's someone else's problem

- Suggest alternative approaches, if appropriate

When it comes to how people experience working with you, complaining is the worst. A complainer can see the problem but only wants to put down others and take no part in fixing it. The second option, assuming that it is someone else's problem, is a bit better, but you get a reputation for not caring. The best is obviously the third choice.

The key to making suggestions for improvements is making sure that people don't feel as if you're trying to indict the way things work now. It's very easy for people to become defensive and resent your attempt to help.

So here's some advice on how to make suggestions for improvements:

- Choose wisely. Don't rattle off everything that needs fixing, just one or two things that will make a difference.

- Acknowledge that you understand that the way things work now has its own logic and that you see that things are this way for a reason, possibly even a good reason.

- Be specific about the experience that made you think about this improvement. When a suggestion comes with the story of the experience that made you think of it, it seems more organic and less as if you are trying to be a know-it-all.

- Reference how this has worked elsewhere, preferably something that you saw firsthand. Referencing material you read can make you seem pedantic if you lay it on too thick.

- Discuss implementation considerations. You don't have to have all the details, but it helps to show that you thought about the work implications.

- Give a sense of the magnitude of the benefit. If you make sure that people have all the decision-making factors in front of them, then it is fairly simple for them to consider the suggestion. If you suggest something without these factors, it can seem like half-baked nattering.

6. Be consistently thoughtful and helpful, regardless of status.

You want everyone who encounters you to have the same experience of working with you. If you only focus on "important people," you get labeled as a suck-up or a self-serving jerk. You're never too old to get labeled as the teacher's pet.

And from a purely self-centered career point of view, you never know who will become a source of a future opportunity. Today's admin may be tomorrow's CEO.

How to comfortably stay top of mind

No matter how good an experience someone had of you in the past, he will bring you opportunities only if he thinks of you at just the right moment.

Do not confuse this with networking. This is not about meeting new people. This is not about trying to leverage a contact to pull strings for you with his powerful friends. This is not about self-promoting. This is also not related to looking for a job. This is not part of a short-term campaign to fulfill your immediate needs. It's part of a long-term plan to advance your career. Here is the rule for being top of mind with people who can help you:

Stay in touch with people you enjoy, respect, or are interested in. Staying in touch with people you like is good, no matter how you slice it. It's good for them, because people like to be liked, remembered, and thought of. It's good for you not only because you may get more opportunities, but also because you'll know more about what's going on in the industry. The more people you keep in touch with, the more you learn.

This is one that we find lots of excuses for not doing. See if any of these sound familiar:

- I'm too busy.

- They're busy and I'll be annoying them.

- They'll think that I'm just trying to get something from them.

- It's been too long and they won't remember me.

- It's been too long and I'll feel bad for not having called before.

- I didn't respond last time they reached out.

- They won't respond and I'll feel bad.

- I don't have an agenda, so I'm wasting their time.

While the list can go on and on, I can say from personal experience that if you reach out to tell people you are thinking of them, they will really appreciate it. Here are some things to remember:

- If they don't respond, it probably has nothing to do with you. They're probably busy.

- They make choices about how to spend their time, and if they call you back, it is because they want to, not because they have to.

- If it's been a long time, they might feel awkward that they haven't contacted you.

- If you feel bad about having not responded to them in the past, just say so.

- Broadcasting on social media is no substitute for personal connection.

Doing this requires scheduling just a little. Don't make a career out of it. Spend about 15 to 30 minutes a week reaching out to people you've worked with in the past. Make it a ritual, the same time and day each week. Here are some ideas for how to reach out:

Ideas for Staying Connected	
Just say hello.	"Hi, just wondering how you are doing."
Say you've been thinking of them.	We launched a new system, and it reminded me of that time we…"
Let them know what's new with you.	"Thought you might like to know we finally got a dog."
Ask an easy question about something they have knowledge about.	"What do you think about this ERP module?"
Look on LinkedIn to see if they've had any life changes and wish them luck.	"Saw that you got a new position. Seems like a great fit. Congratulations and good luck."

This may or may not lead to a phone call or lunch. You may not even get a response. If they read the note or listen to your voicemail, you have done your job. It's possible that neither you nor they want a full-blown reconnection. That's just fine. You're not going to talk to them every week afterward. You're just keeping each other at top of mind, and that will feel satisfying to you both.

CONCLUSION

So this year, don't pay any attention to the endless lists of hot topics and skills. To advance your career, focus on the one thing that isn't going to change. Good relationships create future opportunities. And those opportunities are the raw materials from which your career will be sculpted.

Thinking a bit less about yourself and more about the experience of the people around you is an investment that will pay dividends, both immediate and long term. And you may also be surprised at how much more you enjoy your work when see the happiness you create for others.

GEEK TO MANAGER

This chapter is especially for those of you who are either aspiring managers or are relatively new to your leadership role. It will also be helpful to you if you're involved in selecting and mentoring new leaders. Even if you've been in management for a while, you may have forgotten how confusing this transition can be. It is especially fraught for geeks, who have been trained to do technical work, not to manage people who do technical work.

NEW MANAGERS HAVE NO IDEA WHAT THEY'RE GETTING INTO

This is not meant as an insult. It's perfectly natural. It's not that people are ill prepared for management because of some failure. It's just not possible to really know about management before trying it out.

Whenever someone comes into the job of manager, he has some idea of what it's about. Usually it's based on having watched his own bosses closely. This is a problem. A subordinate's view of a boss's job is inherently limited. What most often stands out in this view is the previous boss's failures. We all know in great detail what we personally hated about our previous boss's approach, especially in how he or she dealt with subordinates.

But dealing with subordinates is only one part of a manager's job. Managers have bigger challenges. They need to manage up to their own boss and sideways to new peers. These relationships are much more subtle and difficult to navigate than can be imagined by the uninitiated.

It usually takes a few years for a new manager to really understand the full nature of the job.

Great engineers are not necessarily great managers of engineers

Promotions are usually handed out for all the wrong reasons. Geeks usually get promoted into management because:

- They did a great job as an engineer.

- They did a great job on their last project.

- Their boss quit and someone needed to step in.

- They volunteered.

Sadly, none of these are good reasons to get a managerial assignment. The best reason to give someone a management job is that he is ready to do the new job, not that he did well at the last job. Otherwise, it's like saying, "Joe is such a good driver, we should just give him a pilot's license and see how he does."

Sure, knowing about the work that your people are doing can be helpful, but it can also be a source of frustration. When a new manager supervises people who are developing and using skills that the manager has spent a lifetime perfecting, he can easily become exasperated when he sees the job being done less elegantly than he would have.

Their first impulse is to think, "Get out of my way and let me do it. It'll take longer for me to explain it to you than to do it myself." Of course, doing this will not only alienate staff, but will also prevent them from growing into the new role.

There's a big difference between being a great engineer and helping others to reach their potential as engineers. And attachment to the former can interfere with competence in the latter.

NEW MANAGERS ARE NEVER PREPARED FOR THE TRANSITION

Transforming from a geek into a manager is much more challenging than just learning about what the job is. It's really a transformation of identity.

Geeks spend their early lives being measured by personal productivity. In school, they are measured by the quality of their papers and their scores on tests. As a technical contributor, they are largely judged by the quality and quantity of technical output. How many modules were coded? How many user tickets got closed? How fast did the servers get installed?

Geeks incorporate all that measurement into how they view and measure themselves. Over time, their self-esteem is driven in large part by how they view their own productivity. "I met my major milestone of coding that module today. So I'm a good person."

But managers need to abandon that lifetime of measurement. They are no longer judged by their personal productivity – the code they produce, the systems they personally fix, or the tests they execute.

They are measured by how productive they make everyone else. Managers *leverage* their own talents rather than *apply* them to the work at hand. As an individual contributor, if you make yourself 10% more productive, that's great. But as a manager, if you can make 15 people 10% more productive, that has a much bigger impact on the organization.

Becoming a manager is about mastering a new identity, about changing how one measures oneself. And it's easy to underestimate how difficult this transition is.

NEW MANAGERS DON'T GET MUCH SUPPORT DURING THE TRANSITION

Bookstores overflow with books on being a manager, but rarely do they discuss the difficult transition of becoming a manager, the subtle shift in measuring one's worth, the struggle to adopt new skills for fostering productivity. It can take a new manager a year or more to begin to appreciate all the things that he doesn't know about the new role *(Hill, 2003)*.

Unfortunately, new managers don't get a lot of sympathy. Can you imagine a subordinate lending a compassionate ear to his newly promoted supervisor? "Well, boss, I see that you're having a difficult time adjusting to all that new power, and I'm sure that pay increase doesn't help much. I imagine that that's tough. I can really empathize with your difficulties. How can I help?" Not going to happen.

New managers never get this kind of support. It's much more common that they get grudging compliance and whispered resentments from individuals who were passed over. Yet it's a time during which they need help more than ever.

So you'd think you'd get some sympathy from your boss, right?

Even though the bosses of new managers have been through the process themselves, they don't often lend a sympathetic ear. Too frequently, managers have forgotten how hard it was and are too busy to think about it. They put new managers in place so that they can delegate work, not take more on.

In effect, new managers lose their old support networks and don't get new ones. Old colleagues become subordinates and don't understand the new manager's challenges. And managers rarely think about new peers as advisors.

New managers require patient supervisors and mentors to survive the trial of the first months in the new role. They need to be monitored and supported during what is inevitably an emotionally trying experience, and they must realize that it is normal to feel stressed, confused, and exhausted during the transition.

FOUR ESSENTIAL SKILLS FOR NEW MANAGERS

To succeed as a new manager, you'll have to unlearn the habits and behaviors that made you successful as an individual contributor. After spending years being rewarded for your personal productivity, you must become adept at entirely new ways of working.

Here are four things you'll need to master:

Letting go of doing

Most technical managers are promoted from technical positions. Often, they were among the best and most productive technical people around. So you'll probably have real trouble letting go of the hands-on technical work. You are good at it. You like it. And it can be really difficult to supervise others who may not be as skilled as you are. You will be challenged by the feeling that it would be faster for you to do something yourself than to delegate it. But you can't be a manager and a technician at the same time. If you won't let go of the old job, you can't embrace the new one.

Knowing what managers do

Many times we've heard new managers say things like, "I want to lead the technology, not the people." Unfortunately, we've never seen a piece of technology that responded to leadership. You lead people, not things or tasks.

Once you let go of all the tasks that you used to do, you might be at a loss as to what activities should take the place of the old ones. You might wonder what value you should be adding to the group, and be unsure about how to productively invest your time. Here are some questions to ask yourself:

- Am I doing work that I should be delegating?

- Do I have a plan to leverage the talents of each member of my team?

- What role am I playing in the difficulties of the team?

- Am I advocating effectively for my team's needs?

- Have I contributed to improving my team's reputation within the organization?

- Am I helping to clarify goals, roles, and processes?

- Have I helped create an environment where the team is eager and excited to do their work?

- Can I explicitly describe my contributions to the team's success?

- Have I identified and nurtured leadership potential on my team?

Measuring managerial success

As a manager, you'll no longer measure yourself by the quality and quantity of what you personally produce, but by the aggregate productivity of your team. You'll have to begin to measure your personal contribution to other people's success. Here are some indicators of successful management:

- Things get done well.

- Problems are not big surprises.

- Issues get resolved.

- Progress continues even when managers aren't there.

- People are engaged with their work and each other.

- Conflict is productive rather than territorial.

- New ideas emerge spontaneously from a variety of people.

Crossing boundaries

Although individual contributors have to deal with people in other departments, the bulk of their time is devoted to working with others in their own discipline. You get used to the language and habits of thought in your own world. You live in an echo chamber. For the most part, geeks talk to geeks, and business people talk to other business people.

When you become a manager, you are suddenly thrust into much more communication with people who are used to distinctly different language and thought patterns. Marketers speak marketing, accountants think in spreadsheets, designers think in pictures. You need to learn to see things from many different perspectives.

And it doesn't stop there. You not only need to understand the myriad cultures, but you need to learn to bridge the culture of geeks and non-geeks. This may be the most difficult of all. A big part of your new responsibilities is to keep these different groups collaborating when they don't really understand one another.

If you are wondering how you can do this, read on. Much of this book is dedicated to helping you bridge geek and non-geek culture. We don't expect you to magically intuit the many pitfalls of this perilous effort. We know firsthand how tricky this part of your new management role is, and we have stocked this book with ample insight to help you become a better bridger.

CONCLUSION

If you are contemplating taking on a management role, go for it. But approach it with some humility and an open mind. Much of the pain new managers experience doesn't arise because the job is bad, but because they expect the job to be different than it really is, or they expect themselves to adjust to it more quickly than is humanly possible.

If you have been in a management role for some time, take a moment to reflect on how the transition was for you. Were you aware of the subtle difficulties described in this chapter? How did you navigate them, and how has that impacted your leadership style?

But whether you are a newcomer to the role or a veteran, it is never too late to let go of preconceptions about what the job should be and who you should be in it. A good place to start in the transition from geek to manager is to appreciate how different this role is from your last one and to be open to the changes in behavior and self-assessment that you need to make in order to succeed.

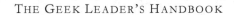

MOTIVATING GEEKS

Among all the topics from Paul's Leading Geeks book, the subject of geek motivation has gotten the most attention and discussion. It's a real favorite. The ideas in this chapter represent an update to the chapter in that book, refined and expanded with more than a decade of additional research, conversation, real-world experience, and Maria's perspective from the other side.

Every technical leader wants a motivated team. Who wouldn't? Motivated teams are more productive than lethargic ones. Motivated teams are more fun to be around. If your team is motivated, you must be a good leader, so it's validating.

There are scads of books written about how to motivate people, so there's no shortage of advice about it. But in our years of working with geeks, we've noticed that much of the traditional advice about how to motivate people doesn't work very well when it comes to motivating technical people.

Geek leaders need their own framework to understand what motivates their teams so that they can create the conditions under which motivation thrives.

In this chapter, we will:

- Explore why traditional techniques don't work with geeks.

- Describe five techniques that work well to foster motivation for geeks.

- Explain how to avoid destroying the innate motivation of geeks.

Traditional techniques don't work for geeks

We've noticed that the vast majority of advice about motivating employees is generic. These books, lectures, articles, and training programs rarely have anything significant to say about the people you would like to motivate. Their underlying assumption is that all people are generally motivated by the exact same things.

Worse, many of the assumptions are based on what motivates people who are vastly different from geeks. If you've been in the work world for any amount of time, you know that salespeople are quite different from software developers. Yet most of the ideas floating around about how to motivate people seem aimed toward the sales types, extroverted and money-driven.

So it's not surprising that the traditional approaches don't work so well for people who are driven by curiosity and knowledge more than money and relationships.

But there's an underlying assumption that is even more of an obstacle to motivating geeks. It's the assumption that you can motivate anyone at all, ever.

You can't motivate someone else

Now, don't worry. We're not suggesting that there's nothing you can do to motivate your technical staff. (Obviously; there's still a lot more to this chapter.) But to be effective, you have to be clear about what motivation is and what you can do to affect it. The link between what you do and how motivated other people are is not nearly as direct as we'd like to think. It's not a simple input/output function. It's not like you drop incentives in a coin slot and out comes motivation.

So the first question is, "What is motivation?"

The simplest definition of motivation is:

Wanting to do something.

And what this looks like at work is that motivated people:

* Feel good about their work

* Invest energy in performing their tasks

* Care about their personal performance

* Feel driven to succeed

* Feel compelled to change the status quo

Looking at this list – feeling, investing, caring – it becomes immediately apparent that motivation is subjective; it is not an objectively verifiable fact. You can't take its temperature or weigh it on a scale or measure it with a ruler. It is a subjective, emotional experience. It's an internal state contained entirely within each individual in your organization. And you can't directly control the inner emotional state of anyone other than yourself (and even that is pretty challenging).

You can't walk into someone's cubicle, stare deeply into his eyes, and say in a hypnotic voice, "You are now motivated. You have energy and drive and commitment," and expect it to work (unless you are Steve Jobs). You can't grab someone by the lapels and threaten to fire him if he doesn't become motivated and expect it to work (unless you are Jack Welch). There is no technique that offers direct control over someone else's subjective inner experience.

The tools you have at your command – rewards, punishment, threats, inducements, and appreciation – may influence someone's inner experience, but they have no deterministic – that is, completely predictable – effect on it. Here's all the evidence you need:

- The same rewards and punishments may elicit entirely different results when offered to different people.

- The same rewards and punishments may elicit entirely different results when offered to the same person at different times and under different circumstances.

So formulaic approaches that claim to offer foolproof motivation are destined to fail.

However, there is one formula that is useful in this realm. The more you know about someone's inner life, what someone personally finds rewarding and punishing, the more you can tailor your actions and the work environment to raise the probability that he will become internally motivated.

YOU CAN CREATE THE CONDITIONS UNDER WHICH MOTIVATION THRIVES

So your challenge as a geek leader is not to motivate people, since you can't directly affect someone else's inner emotional state. Your job is to create an environment in which geek motivation is likely to thrive.

Think of it like gardening. If someone gave you a beautiful, thriving cactus plant, what would you do to make it grow? Well, the truth is that you can't *make* it grow. You can thoughtfully create an environment that is conducive to its growth.

So knowing the nature of cacti would be essential. You'd have to know that they like lots of sun and not too much water, that they need good drainage and occasional fertilizer.

You wouldn't put it in your tropical terrarium, because you know that it would not like the humid and wet conditions. You wouldn't put it in the snowbank in your back yard in January. You would probably pot it in sandy soil, water it once a week, and put it under a high-intensity grow lamp. In other words, you'd create an environment in which the cactus is likely to thrive.

That's your job with nurturing geek motivation as well: to create an environment in which geek motivation is likely to thrive.

There are three key elements to this:

* Recognize the natural motivation that geeks bring to the workplace.

* Create the conditions under which their motivation is likely to thrive and grow.

* Avoid destroying their motivation.

RECOGNIZE NATURAL GEEK MOTIVATION

Let's be clear. Most geeks come to the workplace highly motivated to create and support technology. More often than not, they start out brimming with eagerness, simply for the love of doing great work.

But many geek leaders make the mistake of believing that their people aren't motivated because they display so little emotion. Be aware that they can be highly motivated without your knowing it unless you understand what to look for. If you expect geeks to display their enthusiasm with the same fist-pumping, high-energy, hyperbolic expressions of other people, you'll fail to recognize their excitement and commitment.

And the danger is that if you don't really know how motivated they are, you're likely to inadvertently destroy the motivation they have rather than supporting and expanding it. Motivation is a rather fragile state, and if they sense that you don't believe in their commitment, they can feel misunderstood and dismissed.

To create an environment in which geek motivation will thrive, you need to understand who geeks are and what they find motivating.

WHAT MOTIVATES GEEKS?

Before we get into what specifically motivates geeks, let's ask a more general question about what motivates anyone. Here's a quick rule of thumb to follow when you're trying to create the conditions for anyone to become motivated.

As a general rule, people are motivated to do things that make them feel good or make them feel less bad. This seems rather obvious, doesn't it? But this is exactly what the traditional approach to motivation skips, recognizing that what makes one person feel good might not have that effect on another. And what soothes one person's bad feelings may aggravate someone else's.

What doesn't work with geeks?

Here are some motivational techniques that are commonly used but don't work particularly well with geeks. In fact, many of these tend to backfire and diminish their motivation rather than enhance it.

- *Cash bonuses.* Geeks like money as much as anyone else, but it doesn't engage them creatively with the work at hand. They become motivated to get money, not motivated to do a good job.

- *Unqualified appreciation.* Geeks love to be acknowledged for the amazing things they accomplish, but if you don't have the technical knowledge to understand the beauty of what they've created, your praise seems inauthentic or presumptuous.

- *Parties.* Geeks tend to be introverts and probably don't want to go to a company picnic. They are likely to spend most of their time at the event grumbling about having to give up their private time.

- *Formal awards.* Geeks can be pretty cynical about plaques and trophies handed out by companies. They would prefer the quiet, qualified appreciation of their peers to standing in front of the room and having to smile awkwardly while shaking the boss's hand to receive a plaque.

- *Threats.* Fear can be a great motivator to get people to *do* something you want them to do, but it's rather poor at getting people to *think* creatively and *engage* with their work. You probably wouldn't think of threatening to fire a writer if she didn't win a Pulitzer Prize in the next year, imagining that this would inspire her to new heights of clarity and eloquence.

As you can see, a lot of well-meaning ideas turn out to be ill conceived and ineffective.

What makes geeks feel good?

Every individual is different. Every geek is different. But we have noticed patterns of preferences among people on technical teams, so we offer the following framework for understanding what makes geeks feel good.

Right answers – the search for truth

More than anything, geeks are attracted to solvable problems. Put another way, geeks love questions that have right answers. Most of them gravitated toward math, enjoying the clarity of the questions posed, the black-and-white rules of logic, and the satisfaction of finding the right answer. For geeks, there's almost a spiritual dimension to solving a problem, a feeling that it connects them to something bigger than themselves, to an unambiguous, objectively verifiable truth in the universe.

Probably every geek has had the experience of awe when reaching the end of a mathematical proof. They sat in geometry class watching the teacher prove the Pythagorean Theorem, and as they understood the universality of the theorem, felt a warm glow, a sense that they had just connected with a rare and deep truth.

Some people mistake geeks' quest for truth as a desire to be smug know-it-alls, and certainly there are some geeks who have that quality, but most are simply devoted to finding the truth. They are driven more by an urge to discover truth than they are by a need to prove how smart they are. In case you need evidence of this, watch a group of geeks having an argument about a technical point. You'll see animated and sometimes blunt advocacy for a position, but it's very rare to see geeks defend a position that they no longer believe to be true. Once convinced of their opponent's superior logic, they become fierce advocates for the new truth, rather than defenders of their own disproven dogma.

Challenging puzzles – the drive for mastery

Not only do geeks like to solve problems that have right answers, but they also like those problems to be hard ones. They don't become engaged with simple problems. They are bored by puzzles that pose little challenge. They want to work on things at the boundaries of their abilities, forced to learn new things and to extend their range of mastery. Each puzzle solved represents new conceptual territory conquered and colonized, added to their storehouse of knowledge and sphere of competence.

Have you ever noticed what happens to geeks when you give them easy work to do and extra time to do it? They procrastinate, avoiding the work as long as possible until it finally becomes a crisis; then they complete it with amazing speed. You might think that this is because they are lazy, but that's not usually the case. The reason is that they hate easy puzzles, and at the beginning the work is an easy puzzle. Eventually, the constraints make the puzzle interesting. It's no longer, "How can I write this simple program?" It becomes, "How can I write this simple program in six hours?" Now, that's more enticing.

Meaningful questions – the aspiration to matter

Most geeks also want to make a difference in the world. They want to leverage their knowledge to contribute to the progress of their organizations and the world at large. Just like all people, they are driven to matter to other people, sometimes in small ways, helping only one person at a time, and at others to change the world through technology.

Sometimes, people confuse the tendency toward introversion with disinterest in being a meaningful part of a community. But this is not true at all. Just because you don't want to be around random people doesn't mean you don't care about them. There's little more satisfying to a geek than seeing people using the technology they create or support, then seeing others benefiting from the fruits of their creative labors. It's not unlike an artist watching people in the gallery being moved by her creations.

Here's a rather extreme example. A few years ago I attended a presentation given by the CIO of UNICEF, the United Nations' children's fund. He was describing the work that his people were doing, installing low-speed Internet connections around the world. I found myself imagining the life of the people who worked for him, the modest pay, the repetitive work, 300 days a year on the road, away from their families, to visit some of the poorest and most desolate places on earth, some of them war zones. The facts of the work seemed remarkably unappealing, but it's hard to imagine a job in IT being more meaningful and motivating. Every time one of those new network nodes got installed, a hundred thousand children got to eat instead of starve.

Competition – the pursuit of status

And finally, geeks have the same instinct that all social creatures do to find and better their place in the social hierarchy. Although geeks will frequently tell you that they believe in flat organizations and pure meritocracy, they have as much drive for social status as anyone else. But they measure social status on a scale very different from most people. They generally do not look to money, power, or physical strength. They build their own hierarchies based on what they respect most, such as intelligence, creativity, and work quality.

If you want to see how motivated geeks can be by competition, check out Robot Wars or Punkin Chunkin, where groups of engineers face off in a challenge of mechanical problem-solving. These are battlefields where the weapons of choice are not lances, swords, fists, guns, or bombs. Geeks prefer to fight with neurons.

In fact, many truly transformative technical products were largely the result of intense geek rivalry, fomented by visionary leaders who understood what makes geeks tick. For example, the original Macintosh development team went so far as to move out of the main Apple building, open their own office, and literally raise a pirate flag on the roof, determined to show the rest of the company how much better a product they could build.

CREATE THE CONDITIONS FOR GEEK MOTIVATION

You can use each of these motivators – the things that make geeks feel good – as opportunities to create the conditions under which geeks find their own motivation. The more you can frame your aspirations in terms that they find compelling, the more likely they are to become motivated by them.

Just imagine that you are trying to issue an invitation to geeks that they find so irresistible that they are powerless to resist. Here, we're going to explore five things you can do to appeal to those things that make geeks feel good.

1. Create compelling problem statements
2. Design interdependent roles
3. Build small, focused teams
4. Select wisely
5. Offer free food – but only intermittently

1. Create compelling problem statements

The single most important thing you can do to motivate geeks is to master the art of framing compelling problem statements. This is one technique that you can use to appeal simultaneously to all of the things that make geeks feel good.

There's little more inviting to a geek than a compelling problem statement. After all, for geeks, everything at work, and perhaps everything everywhere, looks like either a problem or a solution. And once a problem has been articulated, geeks feel compelled to solve it.

In the 1988 movie *Who Framed Roger Rabbit*, Judge Doom, the villain, lured the hero, a vaudevillian cartoon rabbit, out into the open by knocking the first five notes of "shave and a haircut." In his hiding place, Roger sweated and grimaced in agony as he tried and failed to stop himself from singing out the last two notes, "two bits." Such is the intense pull a geek feels toward trying to solve a well-articulated problem.

Another analogy: the husband who has been told a thousand times not to try to immediately solve his wife's problems, but to let her "talk about it" as long as she needs to. The desire to just solve it is just too great, and he consistently fails to keep his mouth shut.

You see, everything in technology starts with a problem. How well you articulate it will determine the quality of the technology you get. As consultants, we often see projects adrift, behind schedule, and over budget, with various factions unable to reconcile their competing views of what should be done. In nearly all cases, the root cause of the project breakdown can be traced to the very beginning of the project, when people failed to articulate or build a consensus around what problem the project should be solving. Without that guiding understanding, confusion reigns. And if you want to kill a geek's motivation, confuse her.

On the other hand, a well-crafted problem statement offers geeks a world of motivation. It creates an entire universe for geeks to explore and master. In a few brief sentences, you can:

- Define what it means to win this game (solve the problem)

- Articulate and prioritize goals

- Enumerate key measures of success

- Identify key constraints

- Illuminate values

- Identify competition

- Highlight learning opportunities

Let's look at one of the most famous problem statements of all time, from U.S. President John F. Kennedy's moon-landing speech, which resulted in one of mankind's finest achievements. These few, simple words framed a problem so elegantly that it inspired more than 400,000 engineers for 14 years, consumed 0.4% of the entire United States gross domestic product, and landed a man on the moon. In his speech before Congress, Kennedy said:

> "I believe this nation should commit itself to achieving the goal, before this decade is out, of landing a man on the moon and returning him safely to the Earth. No single space project in this period will be more impressive to mankind, or more important in the long-range exploration of space, and none will be so difficult or expensive to accomplish."

What makes this such a compelling problem statement? Well, let's look at it through the framework of what makes geeks feel good:

- *Right answers.* We want to land a man on the moon and return him safely to the Earth.

- *Challenging puzzles.* No other problem will be so difficult or expensive to accomplish.

- *Meaningful questions.* No other achievement will be so impressive to mankind or important to the long-range exploration of space.

- *Competition.* And the unspoken but not at all subtle subtext that the driving force for all of this is competition with the Soviet Union.

It's no wonder this simple declaration served as such a successful, motivating problem statement for this endeavor.

Now, you don't send men to the moon every day, so you don't always need to touch every motivating factor for your problem statement to be compelling. In a work setting, any one of these alone would probably be enough to create a fertile environment for nurturing geek motivation.

Exercise: Create your own problem statement

Begin by simply capturing the essence of the problem you want to solve with technology. It need not be lofty or exciting, just factual and clear. For example:

> We need to reduce the costs of software testing while improving its effectiveness.

This is a nice, concise, clear statement of what you would like to accomplish. You'll know you've got a good basic statement if it simply frames a problem with a right answer, as this does. It's not inspiring or exciting, but it has the virtue of clarity, which is where you always want to start. Since geeks require a great deal of clarity, never substitute emotional touchstones for clear goals.

Once you've defined the domain of the right answer in a statement, then you are ready to begin layering in the appeals to what motivates geeks. As you can see below, the same basic problem statement can be framed to appeal to any or all of the primary geek motivators. Look for opportunities to highlight:

- *Value.* "We need to reduce the costs of software testing while improving its effectiveness, *to lower the cost of post-release support by reducing the call volume by 10%.*"

- *Difficulty.* "We need to reduce the costs of software testing while improving its effectiveness *in time to test the June 1 release of the product.*"

- *Learning.* "We need to reduce the costs of software testing while improving its effectiveness by *adopting the most up-to-date testing methodology and tools.*"

- *Competition.* "We need to reduce the costs of software testing while improving its effectiveness to make our June 1 release *the highest-quality software the company has ever introduced.*"

With a little bit of practice, you'll be surprised how naturally you are able to frame problems as an invitation to geek motivation.

2. Design interdependent roles

When you plan your projects, you have an opportunity to motivate the team by taking advantage of their natural affinity for one another. Geeks love to help their peers way more than they want to help the boss.

To do this, you need to plan for more than project tasks. You need to provide each person on the project with an explicit role and the goal that defines the success criteria for that role.

Project roles clarify relationships

Geeks on projects need the coherence of a role to guide them in how they execute tasks, relate to other players, and know whether they are contributing or detracting from the collective objectives. A well-defined problem statement clarifies for geeks how they can collectively win the game of a project. Well-defined roles tell them how they can win individually and how their individual success contributes to the larger, overarching goals.

Interdependent roles encourage motivation

Despite what most managers would like to think, people are more loyal to their peers than they are to their bosses. You can think of this as the foxhole mentality of war. Soldiers under fire do not fight for lofty goals, national pride, policy execution, or their commanding officer. They fight to protect themselves and their buddies next to them in the foxhole.

A similar dynamic takes place among geeks on projects. They are not motivated to work 20 hours a day, forgo meals and showers, and abandon their families for weeks at a time to meet a milestone date defined seemingly at random by their project manager. They are motivated to work hard when they know that their own failure will result in harm to their peers.

So when you design project plans and deliverables, you have the opportunity to highlight the interdependence of people on the project by defining deliverables and clarifying the dependencies between team members. The more the team understands explicitly who among their peers benefits or suffers when they fail or succeed, the more motivated they will be to meet their deadlines.

Imagine this common situation. You are a project manager at a meeting with your executive sponsor, and he pressures you to get him a new report by Thursday. You agree to the date and head back to tell your team about their new task. After you tell the developer about the new deadline, she just looks at you incredulously. "There's no way that can be done by Thursday. It will take at least two weeks, and that's if we stop everything else. What were you thinking when you made that commitment without consulting us?" It's unlikely this team will be staying up 24 hours a day to meet the commitment that you made on their behalf.

But imagine if the situation were slightly different. Instead, the deadline had been set long ago, and one developer was responsible for creating the report and the other for creating the screen to launch the report. The developer working on the report is running very late but knows that his friend, the developer working on the screen, can't complete her work until he finishes his. And he also knows that if he is late, she's going to have to miss her child's high-school graduation. In this case, the developer working on the report is likely to stay all night in order to avoid imposing such hardship on his peer.

3. Build small, focused teams

Small, focused teams have a number of significant advantages. They tend to be more creative, productive, and motivated than larger groups with more diffuse focus.

Creativity requires intense focus

Technical work is creative work. We often forget that even the technical work we consider least creative, like support or deployment, is truly creative work. Think about it. Writing code is writing. Solving problems requires imagination and insight. They are nothing like factory work, where you repeat the same process day in and day out. Designing, developing, and optimizing technology demands that you create something that never existed before.

And creativity requires focus. No one is capable of working on five different projects simultaneously and bringing his creative energy to all of them. Team members with too many different projects to focus on find themselves unable to engage creatively with any of their work, and they become discouraged and demotivated. Geeks who can focus on one project at a time have a much better chance of becoming excited to engage in problem-solving with their similarly focused peers.

When you look at the history of transformative technology projects, nearly all of them were carried out by small teams isolated from the rest of their organizations. Besides that Macintosh team that moved to a different building, there's the Data General team that built the world's first 32-bit minicomputer. As described in the Pulitzer Prize-winning book *The Soul of a New Machine*, the team took over a small area in the basement, isolating themselves to focus on nothing but proving themselves better than the engineers in a different facility, who looked down on them. Even open-source software projects seem to be driven by small and passionate groups, even if they have numerous, far-flung contributors.

Mitigate the bystander effect

When teams become too large, they risk falling prey to the bystander effect. Project teams underperform and become collectively passive because each individual team member assumes that things will be done by someone else. Crucial elements may go unaddressed, even if the issues were spotted early by individual team members, because those people thought it likely that someone more qualified or with more authority would take care of it. This happens less on small, focused teams where each person can see what the others are doing and speak up if something is falling through the cracks.

Research into the bystander effect was spurred by the gruesome murder of Kitty Genovese on a New York City street in 1964 and by a subsequent report in *The New York Times* that began, "For more than half an hour thirty-eight respectable, law-abiding citizens in Queens watched a killer stalk and stab a woman in three separate attacks in Kew Gardens." It was reported that none of the 38 witnesses to the crime called the police. At first, it was believed that the neighbors didn't call because they didn't care or were so jaded by city life that they couldn't be bothered to help someone in trouble. But further investigation showed that many of the neighbors who heard the crime being committed didn't call the police because they thought someone else would. Although many years later the initial report was shown to be greatly exaggerated, the bystander effect has been confirmed by numerous studies since then. People are less motivated to help when they think that someone else will, and the effect grows as more people are added to the group of witnesses.

Big teams undermine same-sidedness

Big teams make people feel anonymous. Team members feel like cogs in a giant machine. And no one wakes up in the morning feeling motivated to work his hardest to make insignificant, unappreciated, and unimportant offerings to a distant, giant monolith. If team members feel that no one cares about or truly needs their contribution, there's no reason for them to feel invested in it.

Even if your project is too big to be performed by a small group, you can always break out small teams for subprojects.

4. Select wisely

One of the simplest and most overlooked ways to encourage geek motivation is what we call selecting wisely.

Okay. Stand back and prepare to have your mind blown. Selecting wisely means this: if you want a motivated team, pick people for the team who are already motivated to be on the team.

Think about that for a minute. It seems so ridiculously obvious that we shouldn't have to even write it down. But when technical leaders do resource allocation, they typically forgo this major opportunity and focus on questions like:

- Who's available?
- Who has the skills?
- Who has done this sort of work before?

Of course, these are pragmatic questions that can lead to a conveniently constructed and capable team, but often not a motivated one. Given the choice between a motivated team and a skilled team, we would usually opt for the motivated team, because motivated people will get the skills they need. Skilled teams often plod through familiar territory without enthusiasm or drive.

In order to select wisely, you need to know something about the people you are considering for the team assignments. There are a number of reasons that someone might feel motivated to be on a particular project team. The most common ways to pick motivated people are to:

- *Choose people who find the problem compelling.* They might be attracted to the technology being used, the process being followed, or the benefit the end product offers to the users.

- *Choose people who find their role compelling.* They might be interested in exploring a new role and expanding their knowledge and career prospects.

- *Choose people who find the team members compelling.* They might just want to work alongside the other people on the project.

It's much easier to pick motivated people than it is to instill motivation in people who don't already have it.

5. Offer free food – but only intermittently

Never underestimate the power of free food. We can't offer any definitive explanation, but we have observed that geeks, even those making sizable incomes, will do amazing things for 69-cent donuts.

As best as we can figure, there's something buried deep in the human genetic code that says, "Sharing a carcass is good." If we feed together, we work together.

But the key to this is offering free food intermittently rather than regularly. If you bring in bagels every Friday, it's no longer a motivational perk. It has been transformed into a fundamental human right, and people will only become angry and resentful when the flow of bagels stops.

Bring food when you want the team to come together and feel connected to one another and appreciated rather than when the calendar says it's time to bring the donuts.

AVOID UNDERMINING MOTIVATION

As we mentioned at the beginning of this chapter, geeks frequently come to the workplace carrying their own motivation with them. So one of the most important things you can do to foster motivation in a technical team is to avoid quashing the motivation that's already there.

But though no manager ever sets out with the goal of destroying motivation, it sure happens often enough. Usually, it's the result of thoughtless action that creates the conditions that nurture discontent. Sometimes it happens due to circumstances beyond the control of management.

Your best bet is to be aware of the natural fragility of motivation and to do your best to avoid killing such a valuable thing.

Motivation is fragile

When people feel motivated at work, they care deeply. This is good, right? Don't we want our teams to care about their work and each other? But this good feeling has a potential dark side. Eager and engaged people are vulnerable to the deleterious effects of disappointment. When their efforts fail or are ignored or even mocked, their good feeling can turn mighty sour, mighty quickly. Think of the old saying "The bigger they are, the harder they fall." This principle is true emotionally as well. The more positive you feel about something, the more negative you feel if it doesn't go well.

Let's say that Fred is highly motivated. He's eager to solve the puzzles whose solutions will create great gains for the organization. But then something comes along to undermine his motivation. If you are lucky, Fred will adopt the neutral stance of an automaton, going through the motions of his job. If you are unlucky, Fred will continue to be very motivated, except that he will become eager to scuttle the project and undercut the organization that cruelly dashed his dreams. This is very unfortunate indeed, and not that uncommon. Some of the most disgruntled team members we have encountered over the years had, at one point, the potential to be the most vibrant contributors.

So it becomes essential for you, as a geek leader, to familiarize yourself with the ways that you can inadvertently undermine motivation. These fall into three distinct categories:

- Undermining meaning
- Undermining mastery
- Violating principles

Not surprisingly, each of these is the opposite of the things that make geeks feel good.

Undermining meaning

Here are three common circumstances that undermine a geek's belief that her work is meaningful and important to the organization.

Organizational disinterest

When stakeholders are unwilling or unable to engage in the project, it sends a clear message that the work being done on the project is insignificant. For example, if a developer is working on an enhancement for a report for the CFO and the CFO repeatedly skips meetings, won't respond to emails, won't test changes, or won't approve functional specs, the developer gets the message that the CFO doesn't really care about what he is doing. It's perfectly natural that he feels unmotivated to finish the work. "If you don't care about it, and it's for you, why should I care about it?"

Of course, the CFO is probably very busy and just wants the revised report to start showing up on his desk without any demands placed on him. Part of the geek leader's responsibility is to communicate to the CFO the importance of his participation and the consequences of disengagement.

Underinvestment

All too often, executives demand unrealistic schedules, tight budgets, unworkable features, perfect quality, and spectacular performance all at the same time.

When geeks push to get a more realistic plan adopted and are rebuffed, they throw up their hands in frustration, knowing that failure is imminent and motivation is damaged. "Why try if it's just going to fail anyway?"

And the meaning of the work is suspect, because geeks assume that if it were really important, the organization would be willing to invest realistically to meet the goals rather than sparingly to get nothing.

Exclusion from decision-making

All too often, important decisions about products and projects are made without consulting with the people who are expected to build, deploy, and support the underlying technology. Not only does this lead to faulty products and inefficient projects, but it also undermines the meaning of the work and the meaning of the team's contribution to the work. That is soul crushing. Instead of feeling like valued contributors to the organization, the team members feel that they are regarded as hired help, little more than janitors or plumbers.

As much as their sense of meaning is derived from the importance of their work, it's easily undermined by the sense that they themselves are not considered significant providers of value to the organization. "If they're going to treat me like I don't matter, then I won't let the work matter to me." A geek leader needs to advocate for appropriate inclusion in decision-making if she wants to avoid killing motivation.

Undermining mastery

No one likes to feel incompetent, yet leaders frequently, if inadvertently, convey the message that their people are incompetent.

Excessive monitoring

When geek leaders excessively monitor their team's work – in other words, when they micromanage – geeks feel untrusted and as if their competence has been called into question. Technical people want to be treated as professionals, as experts in their chosen field. When their manager, who frequently knows less about the technology than they do, constantly questions their judgment or expects frequent updates, they get the message that they're not sufficiently trusted or respected to be allowed a reasonable level of autonomy.

Managers who feel completely justified in interrupting a programmer's work every hour for a status update would never dream of calling a lawyer every hour to check which paragraphs he completed in a pending contract. Nobody feels motivated to please someone who displays low regard for him. People are more likely to become petulant and resistant when they feel disrespected.

Unsolvable problems

Nearly everyone in technology has had the experience of a non-technical person displaying outrage at his inability to deliver on an unrealistic expectation. "If I can get email on my iPhone, why will it take a month to get my new report?" Or, "If we can put a man on the moon, I should be able to close the books in less than a week."

Geeks don't like to play games that can't be won, and impossible problems make them feel impotent and resentful. Both are equally destructive to motivation.

Focus on task rather than goals

When there is a problem to be solved, geeks take pleasure and pride in figuring out how to solve it. But if they are told exactly what steps to take, they feel that their competence is being questioned, and their engagement flags.

When geeks are treated like technology vending machines, they feel that their knowledge, expertise, and problem-solving abilities are neither respected nor desired. Not surprisingly, this undermines their motivation by subtly sending the message that their skills are irrelevant.

Violating principles

Geeks are incredibly principled people. Rules and principles provide comforting structure to an ambiguous world, and transgressing accepted rules is very serious business. When principles are seemingly violated for convenience, geeks are at best distracted and at worst enraged. There's probably no faster way to gain the ire and contempt of geeks than to be perceived as inconsistent or hypocritical. Yet, in the real world, circumstances dictate that sometimes you have to break the rules. But be prepared to deal with the fallout and demotivation that results when geeks experience this.

Unfairness

Technical people are deeply committed to the idea of fairness and have very finely tuned unfairness detectors. They prefer a world in which everyone follows the rules and is rewarded fairly for their contributions. If they feel collectively or personally slighted, underappreciated or undervalued, or outmaneuvered, their response is immediate and visceral.

If you see a geek red-faced in anger, it's probably because he feels that he's been unfairly treated. Until he feels that the injustice has been rectified, his attention will be focused on his outrage rather than on what you'd like him to accomplish. And it won't go away. In fact, he's likely to spread his discontent if he feels that his unfair treatment has been dismissed as unimportant.

You see this especially when a geek comes to you asking for a raise. It's rarely about the money. Instead, geeks ask for a raise because they feel that someone else of lesser value is receiving more than them and they must correct the unfairness. Unaddressed, he will seethe in anger until it's resolved or he quits.

Inconsistency

Geeks have an instinctive drive to hunt down and eliminate inconsistencies. That's why so many people perceive them as annoyingly literal and excessively detailed. In software, inconsistencies are called bugs. When you change your mind about things, seemingly vacillating from one principle to another or, worse, applying different rules to similar situations without explanation, geeks will view you as a bug. If you're a bug, they're not motivated to help you.

Changing deadlines

Geeks steel themselves for the intensity of the final push before a deadline, clearing their calendars and warning their families that they will be absent for some period of time. As the deadline for a project approaches, they prepare for battle and expect their boss and other stakeholders to be similarly committed to the deadline.

So when you change a deadline at the last minute, for whatever reason, geeks become upset. You've asked them to sacrifice greatly for something that now seems not to have been that important to you. Once they perceive you as someone who sets arbitrary deadlines and has no regard for their time, they never believe your deadlines again and are unmotivated to meet them.

CONCLUSION

As a geek leader, one of your most important responsibilities is to nurture the motivation of your group; the energy and drive that they bring to their work determines your success. If they are unmotivated, there's little you can achieve. If they're motivated, there's little you can't.

When you let go of the illusion that you can directly control other people's motivation, it frees you to focus your energy on things you can control, things that invite them to feel engaged, things like creating an environment in which geek motivation thrives.

For many of you, this may be the first time you've confronted the fact that, as a leader, you are responsible for things that you cannot directly control, that leadership comes with more interdependence than power.

Don't worry! There will be many more opportunities to confront the feelings of helplessness that come with recognizing the limits of power. One of the best-kept secrets of management is that the higher up you go in the organization, the more dependent you become on the actions and attitudes of others.

But you'll also find great rewards and feelings of accomplishment when you find yourself among your team, a group of people who you've come to know and respect, and you realize that they are excited to come to work, feel fulfilled by their opportunities to learn and grow, and sense that they can contribute in an environment that you've created just for them. If you nurture motivation well, they'll probably never even recognize all the thought and work that you put into making the office feel like a playground. When they are focused on the excitement of their work and the joy of collaborating with their peers, rather than you and your leadership, you will know you've done a great job.

DEALING WITH A

TOXIC TEAM

Sooner or later, every technical leader runs into a difficult, recalcitrant team. Most leadership literature seems to assume that people are open to and expectantly waiting for leaders to take the helm and correct the course. Sorry, but the reality is that some groups are actively destructive and difficult. If you find yourself with one of these toxic teams, this chapter is for you.

Chances are, if you are reading this, you suspect you have a toxic team on your hands, and you're probably feeling pretty bad. You go home at the end of the day feeling wiped out and defeated. You wake up in the middle of the night thinking about something that happened at work and what you should have said. You get up in the morning dreading the thought of going to work. Even worse, as a leader on this team, you know that you should be doing something, but are at a loss to know what that might be.

We have written this chapter because we know firsthand how trying this experience can be, how much it can tax your patience, how it rattles your confidence, and how it contributes to a sense of failure. Leaders of troubled teams often feel completely alone and at sea. So we'd like to assure you that:

- You are not alone. Toxic teams are sadly common experiences.

- There is hope. Teams can be turned around.

- You are not helpless. There are concrete ways of addressing such problems.

So how do you handle a toxic team? First, here's what not to do:

Don't do nothing. The worst thing you can do is to curl up in a fetal position and hope it will all go away. It won't. Without decisive action, toxic teams only get worse and spread their dysfunction to others in the organization.

Don't rush into it. While a sense of urgency is a good thing, it's easy to inadvertently make things worse if you haven't really thought things through.

Instead, we encourage you to consider this adaptable approach to dealing with toxic teams. It is designed to greatly increase your chance of success. Before getting into what to do, it's important that you understand these two essential concepts that underlie the approach.

- How teams become toxic
- Why you need to rethink blame

Then you'll be ready to follow the four-step process for intervening in toxic teams. We'll walk you through the how and why of each step.

1. Find the toxic behaviors and their impact

2. Claim and assign responsibility

3. Choose your interventions

4. Implement and monitor

TWO ESSENTIALS

How teams become toxic

Very few teams start out toxic. They devolve into that state over time. And in order to turn them around, it's important for you to understand how they transform from positive and productive to toxic and dysfunctional.

It always starts with a behavior. And it's not necessarily bad behavior. It's just that someone on the team behaves in a manner inconsistent with the rest of the team's expectations of how things should happen. The triggering behavior may be blatant and enraging or subtle and pass nearly unnoticed.

Perhaps a meeting resulted in raised voices, and the loudest one won the point. Or the developers were left out of the decision-making process and were forced to cut quality corners. Maybe someone on the team was shamed in public. Or maybe the project manager always shows up 10 minutes late to meetings.

The important thing about this behavior is that everyone sees it. It is objectively verifiable and observable. These behaviors then trigger negative emotional responses in the rest of the team. Although most people on technical teams, being geeks, don't express these emotions, they are there nonetheless. Team members seethe with anger at injustice or recoil with shame.

Witnesses to bad behavior come to their own conclusions about what that behavior means. Sometimes these conclusions are merely harsh personal judgments, such as "That guy is an idiot!" Sometimes, more insidiously, these judgments solidify into assumptions about the very nature of the team and the organization. When one person develops negative assumptions, it's a problem for that person. But when they spread to the rest of the team and beyond, they become virulently toxic. Here are some examples of assumptions commonly held on toxic teams:

- It's not okay to be wrong. Mistakes are unacceptable.

- Avoid blame at all costs.

- Excellence is not rewarded. Mediocrity is safer.

- Sharing ideas gets me punished. All management wants is compliance.

- I'm only responsible for technology. People aren't my problem.

- We serve at the whim of ignorant dictators.

- Management doesn't look out for our interests, so we need to take care of ourselves.

- You win here by tearing others down rather than by doing good work.

- Users are the enemy.

- My work doesn't matter.

These toxic assumptions become deeply entrenched and validated when negative behaviors are tolerated and seemingly rewarded. People give Bob what he wants just to make him stop whining. The screaming manager gets promoted. The guy who hides his technical information survives the layoffs when better team players are let go.

What happens next is that the people who were at the receiving end of the behavior respond in kind. They behave in ways consistent with their new, negative beliefs. And that prompts others on the project to reinforce their negative feelings and assumptions and ultimately generate more.

This is how teams become toxic. They transform bad experiences into toxic assumptions through a cycle of negativity. The behavior is the trigger that gets the cycle going. The emotion is the fuel that propels a negative event into an escalating cycle, and the negative assumptions are the toxic vector that spreads throughout the team. Ultimately, these negative assumptions are at the core of what makes a team toxic.

So now we can be a bit more precise about exactly what a toxic team is. Teams with one bad apple are not toxic. Most teams that fail to deliver are not toxic either. And most unpleasant groups are just unpleasant.

A toxic team is one that is trapped in an intensifying cycle of negative behavior, beliefs, and emotions.

The reason that toxic teams are so dangerous is that they infect other teams. Of course, it's a problem if they fail to deliver on their own project goals. But the real danger is in the damage they can do to the organization as a whole. They enlist others in their battles. They share their negative assumptions. And others see the negative behavior being tolerated or even rewarded. This is why you need to act. Toxic teams don't get better by themselves. It's like ignoring an outbreak of Ebola. It starts small but grows fast and is unlikely to stop spreading without thoughtfully targeted interventions.

Rethink blame

As social animals, we seem to be innately wired to want things to be fair and just. It's part of what allows us to trust one another, to band together and collaborate rather than compete. So, instinctively, whenever anything bad happens, our first questions are:

- Who's to blame?
- How to punish them?

And while blame and punishment can be effective in maintaining social order, they are not effective in focusing the creative energy of a technical team. It may be instinctively rewarding to mete out blame and punishment when a team goes off the rails, but it doesn't unleash the potential of the team. Here's why:

Blame focuses attention on the negative past rather than the hopeful future. It engages the team's minds in thinking about the past. They invest their emotional energy in replaying the past, justifying their own behavior, or being outraged by others' behavior.

Blame encourages maladaptive behavior. When people see that being blamed for something is bad, they go out of their way to avoid accepting it in the future. They position themselves, not for the greatest achievement, but to avoid being blamed for failure. They become risk-averse and defensive.

Blame fails to account for the systemic nature of toxic teams. As we will see in more detail later, often the most apparent negative behaviors represent only a fraction of the actual toxic dynamic. Teams don't become toxic by the presence of one bad person.

Blame is particularly painful for geeks. As a group, we geeks see the world through rather binary lenses. You're either good or bad, and we avoid being bad at all costs. Being blamed for something is akin to being labeled a bad human being, and it's quite painful.

To fix a toxic team, instead of assigning blame, you need to focus on accepting and assigning responsibility for behavior and its results.

What's the difference? Responsibility is less about judgment and more about recognizing agency and acknowledging who behaves in ways that need to change. The purpose of acknowledging responsibility is to chart a path to a better future, to find the behaviors that need to be changed. Keep this in mind as we discuss what to do about your toxic team.

4 STEPS FOR DEALING WITH A TOXIC TEAM

So once you realize that you may have a toxic team, what do you do? This simple, four-step process will get you going in the right direction:

1. Find the toxic behaviors and their impact
2. Claim and assign responsibility
3. Choose your interventions
4. Implement and monitor

Our aim in this chapter is not to saddle you with mindless, formulaic steps to follow, but to help you think about your course of action in more detail, to make sure that your interventions target the real toxicity, not just the presenting symptoms. If you follow these steps, you will find that the energy you put into fully understanding the underpinnings of your team's toxicity will greatly increase your chances of turning things around.

Step 1: Find the toxic behaviors and their impact

Make a list of behaviors

Start by listing the behaviors you consider most troubling. Don't try to analyze them yet. Just make a list. It doesn't need to be exhaustive. In our experience, the things that are top of mind are there for a reason. The stuff that keeps people up at night tends to be the things that are most important. To generate a good list, ask yourself or others involved with the team these questions:

- What bothers you most?
- What do people complain about the most?
- What are the excuses people use most?

We recommend that you spend approximately 30 minutes brainstorming a list. Capture these behaviors in a chart, because later you will be analyzing and prioritizing them.

Behavior			
Project manager doesn't share schedule			
Senior engineer explodes during meetings			
Junior engineers never offer opinions			

Analyze the meaning of these behaviors

Once you've assembled a quick list, it's time to analyze it a bit more by asking these questions:

- How does this behavior impact your operations?

- What emotional responses do team members have to this behavior?

- What assumptions arise from this behavior?

Operational Impact

Here you're looking for the direct impact that a particular behavior has on the team. These are the relatively obvious downstream task effects of a behavior that you would see in a project Gantt chart. Here are some examples:

Behavior	Operational Impact
Project manager doesn't share schedule	The test team can't prepare for testing and will either do a poor job or be late. The deployment team can't plan staffing for the rollout, so it won't be able to deploy the system on schedule. The help desk doesn't know when to expect calls about the new system and will deliver poor service.
Senior engineer explodes during meetings	Stakeholders avoid interacting with the engineer. They make less-informed decisions, which leads to poor product design. Meetings are a waste of time because no one says what he really means in order to avoid setting her off.
Junior engineers never offer opinions	Valuable knowledge and insight from people with a newer technology perspective doesn't get incorporated. We waste time coding things in unproductive ways because they don't explore shortcuts or efficiencies.

Emotional impact

But there are also emotional impacts that are not quite as apparent, and it's important to try to understand how this behavior might make people on the team feel.

Behavior	Emotional Impact
Project manager doesn't share schedule	Team is angry that secrecy is tolerated. Team doesn't trust project manager and thinks that he is trying to hide something or game the system. Team members are de-motivated because they feel unable to control their own success.
Senior engineer explodes during meetings	Team is on edge, anxious, and defensive. Team resents her as self-centered and self-indulgent and resists following her lead.
Junior engineers never offer opinions	Team is demoralized and feels disrespected and unimportant.

Assumptions

Once you have described the impacts of the behavior, you're ready to consider the negative assumptions that it creates and reinforces.

For this one, you'll have to use your imagination and sense of empathy. You are trying to imagine what people conclude about the meaning of the behavior. People rarely articulate these assumptions, even to themselves.

You might find this uncomfortable at first. Projecting what other people really think may feel presumptuous, but once you get the hang of it, this will become completely natural. You are not deciding that this is actually what someone thinks or feels. You are hypothesizing based on the evidence available. It might help to view it as an exercise in logical inference. But there's no proof here, just informed conjecture.

Here's how it might look on your chart:

Behavior	Assumptions
Project manager doesn't share schedule	At this company, you can avoid responsibility for deadlines by refusing to discuss them. Management doesn't respect us enough to share plans with us. Management is too incompetent to even have a plan.
Senior engineer explodes during meetings	Basic civility is not respected here. You have to be mean to get ahead here. Decisions here are made based on conflict avoidance more than on logic and analysis.
Junior engineers never offer opinions	Our ideas aren't important. We should just do what we are told. We don't matter.

When you look back at your chart you'll probably start to get a sense of which assumptions are the most toxic. You'll start to see how patterns of negative behavior result from negative assumptions generated by other behaviors. That's how the cycle works.

Priority

Next, you will consider which behaviors, impacts, and assumptions are the most important for you to address. Then think carefully about all that you have uncovered and decide which are the most destructive to the project team and the organization as a whole. You'll discover that some behaviors and assumptions are merely annoying, while others are cancers.

Behavior	Priority
Project manager doesn't share schedule	2
Senior engineer explodes at meetings	1
Junior engineers never offer opinions	3

Once you have gathered all this information and have considered its importance, you're ready to think about who is responsible for the toxicity of the team.

Step 2: Claim and assign responsibility

Earlier in this chapter, we talked about rethinking blame and adopting a more future-oriented approach to claiming and assigning responsibility. Yes, you will need to claim responsibility for much of this behavior. As a leader of the group, you've had a role in creating the problem or allowing it to fester. Your ability to accurately see your part will help you to choose the right interventions and serve as an example to the rest of the team for what taking responsibility looks like.

As we stated earlier, toxic teams are like a broken system. One person cannot be responsible for the team's descent into toxicity. In a healthy team, if one person behaves in ways inconsistent with expectations, that person is either corrected or ejected. Healthy teams have social norms that act like an immune system, rejecting inappropriate behavior rather than allowing it to multiply. Unhealthy teams tend to protect the negative status quo.

So when considering who is responsible for better behavior in the future, consider both direct and indirect responsibility. Direct responsibility is exactly what it sounds like. People who are directly responsible often include:

- The initiator of the negative behavior

- Other team members who respond in kind, or escalate with new negativities

- Leaders who reward it

Indirect responsibility goes to others on the team. While they are not performing the toxic behaviors and directly driving the cycle, they bear a measure of the responsibility. Usually that will include:

- Leaders who tolerate the behavior or fail to put a stop to it

- Team members who imitate the toxic behaviors

- People who encourage it

- People who passively avoid the problem rather than confront it

Here's how it looks on the chart:

Behavior	Direct responsibility	Indirect responsibility
Project manager (Sanjit) doesn't share schedule	Sanjit: He's not sharing the information. Me: I let his bonus go through even though I'm frustrated with his secrecy.	Me: I asked him to share the information twice, but let it slide when he made excuses.
Senior engineer (Sue) explodes at QA lead (Bob)	Sue: It's her temper. Me: I put her in the lead engineer spot even though I knew she had anger management issues.	Me: I just sat there and didn't say anything last time she blew up in a meeting at which I was present. Bob: He is avoiding Sue and hasn't responded to her request to collaborate on test case development.
Junior engineers silent, never offer opinions	Junior engineers: They see looming problems that they don't point out until they become crises. Sue: She scares them with her temper and doesn't ask for their input.	Me: I haven't coached Sue on how to handle junior people, or set the expectation that she needs to grow the talent on her team.

Did you notice how every line item has a "me" in it? It is important that you as leader consider your role in perpetuating the toxicity of the team. It is essential for you to identify what you might have done to encourage it, or how you might have put a stop to it. This will lead you to what you might do differently so that your better behavior will have cascading benefits throughout the team.

Step 3: Choose your interventions

Now you're finally ready to think about what to do – the interventions you want to use to bring the team back from the brink.

What's an intervention?

If you've heard the term "intervention" before, it was probably in the context of helping a drug addict or alcoholic. So you're probably imagining that we are going to recommend that you hold some sort of meeting to confront the people responsible. Don't worry. In this context, the phrase has a much broader meaning. For us, an intervention is simply anything you do to try to improve the situation. It can be as small as setting ground rules for your weekly meeting or as complex as reorganizing the whole organization with multiple layoffs.

As long as you are doing something specific to improve the team's function, then it's an intervention. There are three principles to keep in mind for intervening in toxic teams.

Your intervention should address behavior, not emotions or assumptions.

This may seem counter to what we have been suggesting. We just asked you to do a lot of work to understand how emotions and assumptions fuel the toxic behavior on your team. So it would seem logical that you would try to change the team's emotions or assumptions, right? No. Unless you have been explicitly trained to help people process emotions or change deeply held assumptions, this would be very difficult to do. Perhaps a therapist could effect these changes, but therapists usually have the benefit of working with patients who have volunteered to be helped. Toxic teams rarely ask for help.

Chances are that you would end up doing more harm than good by trying to directly target emotions and assumptions. You've probably witnessed failed efforts to transform teams through mission statements, vision statements, or, worst of all, motivational posters. People just roll their eyes. There is a sense that talk is cheap. If you say, "We value people who are stable team players here," but you just promoted someone with an uncontrollable temper, the team isn't going to believe you. People will only change their assumptions when they see better behavior sustained over time.

And targeting behavior has some inherent advantages. Behavior is objectively observable. Everyone can see it. And everyone expects leaders to set and enforce standards of appropriate behavior.

So your task will be to find ways to modify behaviors that will ultimately transform the team's feelings and their assumptions about the nature and culture of the team itself. By making concrete behavioral changes and replacing dysfunctional behaviors, you will be able to redirect how they think and feel in a more productive direction.

Your intervention must make a forceful, visible, symbolic break from the past.

When a team is suffering in a cycle of toxicity, it needs to be jolted out of it. The intervention you choose has to signify for the team a clear break with the past. Subtle, private gestures are not likely to have that effect. There needs to be no doubt in anyone's mind that the future is going to be different from the past. If there's any room for team members to doubt a better future, they will.

People need to see the better future, not the bad past.

Your team is profoundly aware of the past. Disappointments, insults, and other offenses haunt their thoughts. They are, in their own way, meting out justice for past wrongs done to them. They feel justified and self-righteous about redressing past abuses, and that feels good to them. They will cling to this unless you show them a plausible, nobler future. If they anticipate feeling good about their work and their ability to work with others on the team, they will more easily let go of grievance and retribution.

What are some options for interventions?

So now that you know the underlying principles, what are some actual things you can do? We've organized possible interventions into three categories.

Individual

The least intrusive interventions affect only one individual. They may or may not be visible to the whole team. Individual interventions are nearly always part of the solution, since responsible parties need to understand how their behavior is expected to change. But rarely are they ever the entire solution for a truly toxic team. They might include:

- Holding private conversations with responsible people about their behavior and your expectations for their future behavior

- Hiring a coach to work with an individual on his or her behavioral issues

- Hiring a coach to work with you to help you mentor people with these types of issues

- Issuing threats – HR write-ups, private warnings, etc. – to only one person

- Demoting offenders

Collective

Collective interventions affect the entire group at once rather than one person at a time. Because they are collectively visible, they help establish a shared sense of what behavior is expected. They might include:

- Sending everyone an email about acceptable behavior

- Holding an off-site meeting with the whole team to address team values

- Sending everyone to a training session

- Holding out-of-cycle personnel reviews for everyone

- Establishing formal, written ground rules for acceptable behavior

- Revamping seating arrangements

Structural

The most dramatic and visible of interventions are structural. Changes are made that affect the structure and working relationships of everyone on the team. While these are the most visible, they are also the most risky. They are costly, and you must pay close attention to the meaning you assign to them. They might include:

- Restructuring team roles and reassigning the people who fill those roles

- Firing vendors

- Firing employees

- Canceling the project entirely

What to do with the bad apples?

This is one of the toughest questions in dealing with a toxic team. There are bad apples. People may be individually productive but make everyone around them so miserable that the entire team becomes less productive. In thinking about what to do with these people, assess whether their negativity is situational or the result of something more intrinsic to their nature.

If you think it's situational, consider:

- Placing them in a role that better fits their temperament and talents

- Removing them from the project and assigning them elsewhere

- Keeping them on the project but isolating their work from that of others on the team to reduce their influence

- Physically isolating them so that they are in less regular contact with everyone else

But there are a few reasons that it may be necessary to just fire them, such as:

Incompetence – Let's face it, some people get put in positions that they are ill equipped to hold.

Character flaw – Sometimes people are just too damaged to work with. They may have problems that you can't fix, like pathological lying, excessive stubbornness, intolerable arrogance, or uncompromising selfishness.

Inability to change – Sometimes people have significant flaws that might be fixable but not in a time frame consistent with being part of your organization.

How you deal with such people will send a message to the rest of the team. If you deal with them leniently, the team may learn that the organization is benevolent and gives employees the benefit of the doubt. Or they might conclude that no one is willing to make tough decisions to protect them. You'll need to frame things carefully no matter what you decide.

Step 4: Implement and monitor

The success of your team will depend on how well you implement the interventions you choose. We offer the following advice to increase your chances of success.

Enlist support of key players in advance.

Make sure to talk to the influencers within the group about your planned course of action. You need their support to make the intervention work, and you'll want to gauge their response. They might see something that you missed in your analysis or detect something off-putting in your approach. Where human resource policy allows, give them a chance to help improve the intervention.

Take appropriate responsibility.

Taking responsibility may be the single most important thing that you can do to prevent the intervention from turning into a finger-pointing match. In doing so, you are setting an example and making it safe for people to admit they have made mistakes. By publicly acknowledging your part, you demonstrate your recognition that team situations are complicated, that people make mistakes, and that mistakes are forgivable when new behaviors are adopted consistently.

Focus on the future.

Everyone knows that things have gone off the rails. Focus on what you want to happen in the future rather than what you don't want. Your discussion should not be a long list of what people won't do anymore. It should focus on what they will do.

Acknowledge emotions to diffuse them.

Emotions do not respond to mechanistic fixes. You can't just tell people to feel differently than they do. But, happily, emotions behave in fairly predictable ways, and the easiest, most sure-fire way to soothe hurt feelings is to simply acknowledge them with a bit of empathy. Here's an example of what you might say:

> "I know that a lot of you have felt frustrated and insulted by our team's habit of not sharing information. I know exactly what that's like. I've experienced that in other situations. I'm really sorry that this has been so painful and unnecessary."

A simple statement like this can go a long way toward diffusing negative emotions. This process may seem almost like magic because so little is actually done. But it adheres to a tried-and-true principle of trust and belonging, which states:

If you feel on the inside the way that I feel on the inside, then I can trust you to understand me and treat me with care and respect. I can trust that we really are on the same team.

If you invest even a small amount of your attention during the intervention to diffusing negative emotions and bolstering belonging in this way, you increase your chances of a successful intervention.

Clarify what's acceptable and what's not.

As the leader of the team, you are expected to establish norms and correct behavior. Otherwise, the bullies win. Just as a parent would remind her child not to chew with his mouth open at the dinner table, the group leader sets the boundaries of good behavior with both praise and correction. She uses statements like:

"We don't yell at each other on our team. That is not acceptable."

"It's not okay to sit on information that other people need and not share it."

"Thank you for letting us know in advance that you would be late. That shows the kind of respect we all need to show for one another's time."

These statements are the very stuff of what it means to lead people out of toxicity. Framing them in simple terms is exactly right. It may seem that you are treating people like juveniles, and you are. Until the rules of acceptable behavior are internalized by individuals on the team, you need to speak them out loud, in no uncertain terms, whenever they are transgressed.

You might consider publishing a set of ground rules. If you can do this credibly, back them up consistently, and hold yourself accountable to them, then ground rules can be an excellent tool.

Focus on principles.

When you state what is acceptable and what is not, you can accelerate the adoption of new assumptions about the team by emphasizing the principle that you are committed to. For example:

"We don't raise our voices to each other, because on this team we owe one another basic professional respect."

"It's not okay to hoard information, because on this team we help one another do our best work."

Follow up relentlessly.

Consistency is key. It will take quite a while for people to believe that things will really change for the better. Do not make exceptions, and do not allow your attention to be diverted from the details of this behavioral change. It took a while for things to get bad, and people will need to see more than a few days of correction from you. If your determination to enforce the new standards ebbs in any way, people will be quick to label the whole effort as an exercise in hypocrisy and futility, and all of your work will be for nothing.

How will you know if it's working?

How recovery happens

Not surprisingly, recovery is the reverse of the toxic cycle. If you've chosen your interventions well and delivered them with sufficient force, the result will be an immediate shift in behavior. Over time, as the cycle repeats, the old, dysfunctional assumptions will be replaced by better ones, leading to better behavior and better assumptions still.

As you continue to enforce the new standards, you also need to monitor the team for signs of progress or backsliding. If you see progress, make sure to recognize and reinforce it. If you see stagnation or further descent into toxicity, you'll need to act quickly to implement more significant interventions.

Early signs of trouble

Here are some common signs that your interventions are not having the desired effect:

- Nothing changes

- Turnover accelerates

- Bad behavior escalates

- People complain that intervention is insufficient

- People complain that the responsible people haven't changed their ways

If any of these come up, you'll need to consider your next move quickly. And you should seriously consider getting outside help. These problems are hard for anyone to solve, which is why there are battalions of consultants devoted to helping people in exactly your situation.

Early signs of success

Hopefully, you'll start to notice signs of progress, signs that the group is moving in the right direction. Look for things like:

- People thanking you for intervening

- People showing a visible sense of relief

- Creative energy getting focused on the project rather than the problems

- Disagreements being about the substance of work rather than personal hostility

- Turnover reduction

- Less time being devoted to private, whispered conversations

If you see these things begin to occur as a result of your efforts, go ahead and feel good about it. Your good feeling will be infectious and will serve to accelerate the team's transformation.

You'll know you really succeeded when:

- Responsibility is accepted, apologies happen, and mistakes are forgiven

- Ideas, insights, and suggestions flow freely and are respected

- Information is shared and advice is sought

- Credit is shared, people thank each other, and successes are celebrated together

- Feedback is constructive, is naturally occurring, and assumes good intent on all sides

- Help is asked for, offered, welcomed, and reciprocated

- Lively disagreements lead to better solutions

- People smile, laugh, and get excited about work

CONCLUSION

When you started reading this chapter, you probably had a dark cloud of dread and confusion hanging over you. There are few things in life more damaging to one's confidence and sense of self-worth than being on a toxic team. And there are few things more daunting than trying to turn one around. The steps outlined in this chapter will take a significant amount of focused attention, imagination, creative problem-solving, and courage. But we believe that these steps are your best hope for transforming your team. If you're committed enough to seek out and read this chapter, you are exactly the person your team needs.

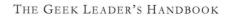

SHAPING FUTURE
TECH LEADERS

We have noticed that in the urgent, day-to-day business of delivering and supporting technology, geek leaders often lose sight of the satisfying and enriching enterprise of identifying and developing the skills of the next generation of technical leaders. This chapter focuses on the importance of nurturing new leaders and provides insight into how to do so effectively.

Paul and the CIO

It was a beautiful afternoon. My former client and I were lingering over our lunch as we looked out over the water and enjoyed the breeze of a particularly mild day. He was a CIO, just about to retire, and he was in the mood to reminisce. He talked about the technology he had seen come and go. He pondered the differences in the three large organizations he had served. He predicted what he would miss and not miss about being a CIO.

And as the conversation meandered pleasantly onward, he hit upon a topic that really lit him up. He became animated and alive. He actually seemed to swell with pride when he began to talk about the people he had mentored, some of whom had become CIOs, making a difference in their industry.

It was clear that what mattered most to him were the people he had developed into successful tech leaders.

Making a lasting impact

Most technical leaders enjoy the thrill of meeting the demands of an ever-changing industry. In our environment, nearly everything is urgent. Change is constant. Technologies come and go. Processes, organizational structures, job descriptions, and titles all rotate through a Mixmaster of constantly shifting fads. And usually, we love it.

But for many managers, there's a less appealing side to this coin – the sense that nothing lasts, that everything we do rapidly turns to dust. There's a sadness that comes with the realization that all our work can be swept away in a matter of months.

So that leaves us asking, "What can we do to have lasting impact on our organizations and industries?"

The good news is that you *can* leave a lasting mark, and there's probably someone who can help you sitting somewhere outside your office door right now. You make an enduring difference through the people you choose to develop.

Selecting future tech leaders

But whom should you choose to mentor? The most common mistake we make when selecting people to mentor is picking our favorite people to work with. We might like working with people because they are smart, effective in their role, committed to getting things done, or just fun to be around. Or maybe we just like them because they minimize negative drama.

However, these are not necessarily the things we should be looking for in future leaders. In fact, there are several commonly held misapprehensions about what traits to look for in selecting technical leaders. Let's take a look at some.

Poor predictors of leadership success

Technical genius

It's natural to assume that people with strong technical skills would be able to leverage those talents to enhance the productivity of everyone around them. Alas, it rarely works out that way. Technical skills are not an impediment to being a good manager, but neither are they all that transferrable. The ability to translate one's own personal knowledge into other people's productivity is rather rare. Most technical gurus don't know exactly how they do what they do. Native skills are hard to describe and teach to others.

And the traits that go into making someone a technical wizard might be exactly the same traits that make a mediocre manager. For example, technicians need the ability to focus on one thing for long periods of time, but managers need to be able to shift focus or multitask constantly to be successful in interruption-prone managerial work.

Education

We tend to put a lot of stock in education, and the more advanced the degree and prestigious the school, the better. While education does indicate something about the person who holds the credential, rarely does it mean what we think it does. An advanced degree might indicate persistence more than brilliance. A degree from an elite school might indicate raw intelligence but not necessarily hard work. We can't count the number of times we've worked with highly credentialed project managers who get so enamored with perfecting a theoretical process that they accomplish nothing.

The biggest misperception is that an MBA prepares people to manage. MBAs have been trained to think about businesses analytically but not necessarily how to lead people to deliver things. And when engineers get MBAs, it's like doubling down on analysis. Education can tell you a lot about the person you are evaluating, but you need to question whether those traits are really leadership traits.

Dominating personality

The desire to lead is not necessarily a good indicator of someone's ability to do it well. In fact, when it comes to leading geeks, the desire to command and control is usually counterproductive. Technical people need to be led by someone who wants to help them succeed rather than someone who wants to be in charge. Geeks have finely tuned blowhard detectors and resist being told what to do by someone who is trying to gratify his own ego. Geeks can tell when someone feels secure only in a dominant position, and they scorn that person for it.

Charisma

We all like to be around people with charisma. They make everyone around them feel special, but this isn't necessarily the right quality for making a group of geeks more productive. Charisma can be a great tool if someone knows what to do with it, but too often charismatic people spend their lives being rewarded for being charismatic and may miss out on experiences that lead to emotional maturity.

In fact, charisma often masks significant deficiencies that only show up after a person has been given a leadership role. Some naturally charismatic people develop a sense of entitlement in response to the adoration heaped on them throughout their lives. They rely on their natural likability to influence others, without learning to build coalitions based on what other people need and desire. Charisma can be a liability when managing technical teams, since geeks respond to reason and are naturally suspicious of charm.

Good predictors of success

So if a number of common signs of leadership potential are misleading, what are good things to look for?

Emotional flexibility

Perhaps the most difficult thing to find among engineers is emotional self-awareness and flexibility. But this may be the most important skill a manager can have. They need this for two reasons. First, the transition into management is very difficult and often personally wrenching. Successfully navigating this transition requires the ability to be reflective and accept change.

Second and more importantly, emotional flexibility is a requirement for being a good leader. Good managers are aware of their own emotions but don't necessarily act on them. They have to choose what to express and when in order to help their people be productive. A manager who is unable to navigate his emotional responses can't provide the stability and guidance that others need. Managers who can put the emotional needs of their staff ahead of their own emotional needs tend to be better at finding the solutions with the best fit and keeping team members engaged and motivated.

So how can you spot emotional flexibility? Emotionally flexible people tend to:

- Take criticism well; don't easily take offense

- Reflect positive emotions such as eagerness and enthusiasm

- Resist succumbing to a group's negative emotions

- Take care to word things so as not to cause offense

- Stay calm when others don't or can't

Comfort with ambiguity

Reality is a messy business. A big part of the manager's job is to make sense of the world so that others can navigate it successfully. Good managers help create a coherent understanding of projects and processes, of goals and strategies, of politics and constraints, so that other people are not paralyzed by indecision in the face of confusion. They need to be able to create a sense of coherence so that others can be productive.

This often requires knowing which ambiguity to resolve and which to leave open. But for geeks, this is a rare skill. Engineers are drawn to concrete work in part because of their discomfort with ambiguity. Geeks who want to manage other people need to develop a tolerance for ambiguity and for actively managing it rather than reacting to it instinctively.

What does it look like when people are adept at managing ambiguity?

- They tend to organize what is known and not known into actionable categories

- They are productive in the face of of ambiguity

- They help others to be productive in the face of ambiguity

- They ask questions that help others clarify the current degree of ambiguity

- They consider the reason certain information is needed and prioritize it accordingly

Other-focused communication

A manager's primary job is to make other people more productive. If an artist works in oils or watercolors, a manager works in people. No matter how smart he is, no matter how grand his strategies, wise his decisions, or clever his tactics, he can't be effective if he can't get other people to do things. And the only way to get other people to do things is through communication. If he can't clearly and compellingly communicate a way forward, his genius is of no use.

Effective communication isn't just expressing oneself clearly. Communication is effective when each audience member understands the ideas and the meaning that the communicator intends to transmit. This means that managers need to have a strong sense of the other, because each person hears differently through the lens of his own experience and presumptions.

To penetrate those filters, managers need to have a strong sense of how other people see the world. Then they use that understanding to adapt their communication to the needs of each person.

If you want to spot someone with other-focused communication, look for someone who:

- Listens more than talks

- Notices when someone is confused, upset, or tuned out

- Can deliver the same message in different, nuanced ways

- Shifts modes of communication as needed: meeting face-to-face, drawing on a whiteboard, writing a detailed summary

- Uses verbal cues of understanding: "I can see how you came to the conclusion ..."

- Writes emails that are concise and easy to say yes to

MENTORING FUTURE LEADERS

Now that you know more about whom you might want to mentor, let's talk about what you can do to help them.

Find out about them

Learn about their aspirations. The first thing to do is to figure out if they already have ideas about what they'd like to do with their careers. While they might have thought about becoming a technical manager, they may have completely different aspirations. If a prospective mentee is already set on going to medical school, she might not be a good candidate to be your mentee.

Find out how they think about management and leadership. Before you start laying out any plans for how you're going to develop your mentee, you need to understand her starting point. You'll need to probe to find out what she thinks about managers and management, and whether she pictures herself in those roles.

Here are some questions you can ask to get started:

- "Tell me about the best manager you've ever worked for."

- "What made this person such a good manager?"

- "Who was the worst manager you ever worked for and what made him or her especially difficult?"

- "What would you have done if you had been in the role of your favorite or least favorite manager?"

- "What do you think is the most frustrating part of being a manager?"

- "What do you think is the most difficult part about being a manager?"

Ease into it

Once you have a sense of your mentees' mental starting points on the journey to becoming a manager, you can start to lay out specific things you'd like to work with them on.

Don't make anything official. The moment you designate someone publicly and officially a management trainee, his relationships with his peers and supervisors change. There are new expectations and alienations. You want to give him an opportunity to learn and experiment without the added pressure of shifting relationships.

Find opportunities for them to practice. In small, limited ways, give them an opportunity to experiment with managing their peers. As a task leader, they'll have the opportunity to try on the role without having all the pressure of the position.

Make it safe for them to say, "No, thanks." Another reason to allow them to experiment is that it buys time for them to decide whether it's a role that they're interested in. A large percentage of engineers who take on managerial roles discover that they don't like them. Here's why:

- They're disappointed by the mismatch between their expectations and the reality of management.

- They discover that the loss of the technical work is too painful.

- They fail to navigate the shift in self-image that's required to become a manager.

New managers who decide they want to go back to being individual contributors after accepting a formal title frequently leave the company. They can find no way to go back to the role that they crave without feeling humiliated. And so companies lose some of their best talent when excellent engineers decide that they would rather be geeks than managers.

Gradually increase their load. Creating practice opportunities also gives you the chance to observe them in action, checking whether your assessment of their potential was accurate. It gives you the chance to decide whether you've made a good choice without either you or them losing face. If you feel that a mentee is ready for a real challenge, take a vacation and leave him in charge. When you come back, you both will have learned a lot.

Help them develop management skills

The chapter on "Geek to Manager" identifies a number of skills that technical people need to master. There are a few things you need to know in order to help them do so.

Avoiding common mentor mistakes

Sometimes it's hard to get started with mentoring other people.

Here are a few common challenges:

Being overly humble – "Who am I to teach someone what to do?" This abdicates responsibility. If you have achieved a certain level of success, you must follow Spider-Man's motto: "With great power comes great responsibility," even if you're not quite sure you deserve it.

Making a Mini-Me – Develop *their* talents. Don't try to turn them into a clone of you.

Taking disappointments personally – Not everyone will succeed. So don't let setbacks get you down.

Overlooking the "obvious" – Never assume that what's obvious to you is obvious to someone else. If common sense were common, there wouldn't be any problems in the world, right? Get in the habit of double-checking things that you assume they already know.

Getting distracted – Just because you have a busy job doesn't mean you can ignore the people you are trying to develop.

Expecting them to come to you – They want to respect your time and probably will be afraid to bother you, so you need to be explicit about making time for them.

Give them articles and books

As you choose things for them to work on, every once in a while pick one article or book for them to read. This gives them a sense of what you feel is important they learn about. It also gives them the opportunity to explore perspectives from many different people. After you've had them read something, make sure that you follow up with them and have a discussion about it. Find out what they absorbed or learned and whether they agree with it or not.

But don't overwhelm them with too much reading material. If you give them one or two articles to read, they'll treat them with great care, since they represent something of a gift. If you assign an entire shelf of books, it will start to feel like a chore that reminds them of excessive homework.

Allow them to make their own mistakes

You need to make sure that you are not teaching them to be too dependent on you. As a coach, it's easy to fall into the trap of being the wise advisor. This doesn't train people to think for themselves, but to become dependent on you.

You also need to recognize that people learn much more from mistakes than they do from success. If you prevent them from making too many mistakes, they won't learn very much. All that will happen is that they will think they know more than they do about how to navigate the managerial role. At some point when you're not around, they'll discover how little they know and will likely react badly.

When they do make mistakes, don't be too judgmental. But do insist that they learn from the mistakes. Engage them in discussions to clarify what went wrong and how to avoid it in the future.

Ask questions instead of telling them what to do

Have you ever noticed that telling people what to do is a remarkably ineffective way to teach them anything? Do you remember feeling empowered and energized by a long lecture when you had done something wrong? Probably not.

When you make a statement, the other person, at best, evaluates it. If you want to teach people to think for themselves, then focus on asking questions rather than giving answers. Ask someone a question and he will begin to think about how to answer it.

And the more open-ended the question, the better. Notice the difference in your mental experience when you read the following two bullet points. Read the first and then pause a moment before reading the second.

- How can you tell if the project you're working on is in trouble?

- Do the earliest signs of project problems appear in the relationships within the team or between the team and the business sponsors?

Which one made you think more?

When you become skilled at questioning, you can lead people where you want them to go and make them feel like they took you there.

Emphasize values and principles

The last thing to consider (though some would aptly argue that it should be the first thing) is the values and principles you embody and reinforce. Too often, managers think that their values are transmitted in the words they use, the explicit statements they make about what they believe and feel are important. But nothing could be further from the truth. People don't absorb values from mission statements, values proclamations, or inspirational posters.

People learn about your values by:

- How you behave
- How you treat other people
- What you pay attention to
- What you reward
- How you react in crisis situations

In other words, they learn about your values from those you embody in your everyday interactions, not from what you espouse.

That is why people hate moralistic proclamations from managers. Very often, the hypocrisy is too much to bear. You've heard a manager say something like, "We value your input, and my door is always open." But when you knock on his closed door to offer some input, you're greeted with a blank stare.

As a mentor, you have an unparalleled opportunity to impart the values you feel are important. But to do that, you'll need to know what your values are.

Chances are, you haven't really tried to explicitly describe your business values. For most of us, they evolve silently and remain unexamined.

But you can figure them out through honest reflection. Your behavior is already consistent with your values. So start out by honestly reviewing your own behavior. (If your behavior is not aligned with your values, chances are that you are miserable in your job and probably looking for a new one rather than thinking about mentoring other people).

Of course, it might not be so simple. It might be somewhat sobering, but with a bit of work, you will find the language that ties what you do and how you do it to what's really important to you. You will need those words to pass on your values to other people. When your words are consistent with your behavior, you maximize your ability to impact other people.

MANAGE THE MEANING OF THE PROMOTION

When and if your mentee gets a formal promotion to management, you need to set him on a path for success. Hopefully, by the time he gets the official promotion, you've already prepared him with your mentorship. But there are two more things you can do to set the stage for his success.

Ritualize the transition

Marking transitions such as managerial promotions is good for everyone involved. For new managers, rituals symbolize the official sanction of the organization. But they can also reinforce the sense of transition. Rather than just ordering a cake and having a 15-minute gathering in the lunchroom, maybe you could have a "formal" surrendering-of-the-sliderule ceremony. For everyone else, it gives them a chance to recognize the clear shift in role of their old peer. They now must adjust to the new responsibilities and roles.

Set them up for success

The other thing you can do is to be explicit with the organization about why the new manager deserves the promotion. Be clear about this person's capabilities, character, behavior, and values that led him to be selected for this new role. It communicates more clearly than you can imagine what the organization really cares about.

VALUING YOUR ACCOMPLISHMENT

There are two distinct ways to think about the value of mentoring: organizational and personal.

How mentoring benefits your organization

It's important to have a good understanding of how your mentoring efforts help your organization. After all, you usually do it on the clock, and like anything you do on the company's dime, you should be prepared to defend the time you devote to it.

First, you are helping to increase your group's productivity, since good leaders make the people around them significantly more productive. A leader who manages ambiguity, prioritizes activities, eases difficulties, and overcomes obstacles helps everyone get more done. Mentoring new leaders seeds the organization with people who raise productivity.

Second, you are opening up your availability to contribute at a higher level. Assuming that you are savvy and strategic and your insights bring value to the organization, growing new leaders frees you from tactical management tasks and allows the organization to leverage your most valuable skills.

Finally, in shaping leaders, you are shaping the culture of the organization in positive ways. You are creating an environment where people feel valued. By mentoring just one future leader, you are sending signals to their colleagues that this is a place that creates opportunities for future growth.

You still have to find ways to talk about the value of your mentoring efforts to your boss and your colleagues. It can take the form of describing your efforts in your status updates. It might go something like this:

"I've been working with Jim so that he is clear in setting expectations with the team. In the past we've ended up with duplicate work because he wasn't clear enough with the group about who should be working on which piece of the system. We've done some exercises in our one-on-one meetings that have really helped. In the six weeks since we started working on this, his team has reduced the amount of throw-away code by about half."

By finding ways to be explicit about the fruits of your mentoring efforts, you can help ensure that you and your team will get appropriate credit for good work. In this way, you can allow yourself to serve as an example and resource for your peers who may have people of their own that they want to develop.

HOW MENTORING BENEFITS YOU

But we don't mentor people only because it's part of the job description. We do it because it's valuable for the people we mentor and fulfilling for us.

So imagine that it's many years in the future and you and a friend are having lunch in a restaurant overlooking a beautiful lake, reflecting back on your career. And your friend asks you, "What are the things you did that you are most proud of?"

You take a deep breath, put your hands behind your head, and think back over your long and satisfying career. It's hard to choose among all the things you've accomplished. After a few moments of reflection, you answer with confidence, "I'm most proud of setting Bob, Sandy, and Sanjay on the path to success. I was the first to spot and develop their talents. Not only are they great leaders, but they are passing on what I gave them to the next generation of leaders." Your friend congratulates you, and you both raise a glass to a career well spent.

PART III

Working with External Stakeholders

ESTABLISHING

NEW CLIENT

RELATIONSHIPS

There are a few key moments in a relationship with a client or a stakeholder that make all the difference in the relationship's long-term success or failure. One is at the very beginning, and as the old saying goes, you only get one chance to make a first impression. Although this chapter was originally written as a white paper for external service providers, the insights and advice in it apply almost identically when establishing relationships with new internal stakeholders.

Landing a new client is both exciting and terrifying. You've put a lot of effort into the sales process, and it has paid off. The contract is signed. The rates are negotiated. And the statement of work is completed. Now all you have to do is deliver, right?

Wrong.

We believe that the conventional wisdom about how to get started with a new client is entirely inadequate. Most of the advice you'll find boils down to a single, simple idea:

Demonstrate your value by delivering a "quick win."

If the client sees you delivering what he asked for early and often, you'll look like a star and become a "trusted advisor" whom the client will come to for help again and again.

While there is some value in this advice, it is dangerous. It fails to capture what's really important in establishing a relationship with a new client. It results in disaster as often as success. Whether you've been hired as an independent contractor, a temp-to-perm, or a member of a large consulting team, if you put just a little extra attention into establishing a relationship, you can positively influence how the client views you. You can prevent yourself from becoming a faceless drone supplying commodity tasks and instead become a go-to member of a client's inner circle.

Paul's story of hapless Jerry

A few years ago, I worked with Jerry, a very capable consultant who started a client engagement hell-bent on a quick win. The CIO brought him on to write a requirements document for a custom application to extend the company's internal financial system. Within two weeks, Jerry had the first section of the document done. The CIO loved it, and with good reason. As far as documents go, it was shaping up to be a work of art. It was clearly written, lucidly structured, beautifully detailed, and represented multiple perspectives. Honestly, it was on track to become one of the best requirements documents I've ever seen, and I've seen a lot.

Jerry passed the quick-win test with flying colors.

So he buckled down and continued to produce similarly impeccable work, and at the end of three months, he dropped a 130-page masterpiece on the CIO's desk. It was exactly what had been asked for, but within a week Jerry was let go. His services wouldn't be needed any longer. Instead of a lucrative, multiyear engagement, Jerry was out hustling gigs again.

What happened? The CIO had sat down with the CFO to review the document to get the go-ahead to implement the project, but instead of giving the expected endorsement, the CFO was incredulous. He said that they didn't need anything that elaborate and expensive. He just wanted a simple solution. So the project was canceled.

How did this happen to Jerry? Was it just an unlucky break? Are fickle clients just an occupational hazard?

No, on both counts. Jerry was a victim of the quick-win theory. Had he focused his early attention on building a relationship with the CIO instead of being single-mindedly devoted to delivering on the specific request, he might still be working with that client today.

THE MYTHS OF THE QUICK-WIN

The quick-win theory of early client engagement is an appealing one. On its face, the theory makes sense. You want to establish trust quickly. But the quick-win approach to earning that trust is based on two fatally flawed assumptions that undermine its effectiveness:

Myth 1 – Clients want what they asked you for.

Myth 2 – You build trust by demonstrating competence.

To establish a lasting relationship with a new client, you need to replace these myths with some fundamental truths.

Myth 1: Clients want what they asked you for

You'd like to think that clients know what they want. You'd like to think that the statement of work in the initial contract is a true picture of what will give clients what they want. But the regrettable truth is that even though clients might know what they hope to accomplish, they can't know what they need technically.

Here's why:

Clients lack the technical knowledge to know what they need. If they really knew all the technical details of what should be done, why would they hire you? You're supposed to be the expert. You probably wouldn't feel too comfortable if you went to visit your primary-care physician and he blankly stared at you, waiting for you to tell him what procedure to perform. You expect your doctor to tell you what should be done based on the symptoms you describe.

You learn as projects progress. Over time, you and the client learn that your initial assumptions were wrong. The tasks in the statement of work may prove unworkable. The proposed solution may have no real relationship to the desired outcome. The client may have failed to account for all the variables in need of prioritization. Those may be technically infeasible, prohibitively expensive, or untimely. What a client initially asks for represents a best guess, based on the limited information available to the client at the time of first meeting you.

What clients explicitly ask for is usually a presumed solution to an unarticulated problem. Not only do clients not know the specific technological solution to their problem, but they often haven't articulated the problem they want to solve. They have a strong sense of what they want to accomplish, but it hasn't been clearly spelled out in words. They have some goal in mind when they hire you, but often the sales process bypasses the difficult task of truly clarifying it. Everyone assumes that they all have a common understanding of the goals, so they don't bother to discuss it.

Think about Jerry for a minute. He delivered exactly what the CIO asked for, a spectacular requirements document. But it turned out that the document didn't really solve the underlying problem. The presumed solution of an extension to the financial system wasn't aligned with the unarticulated issue that had to be addressed. All the CFO really wanted was a simpler way to import data into the system. If Jerry had helped articulate the underlying problem, everyone involved would have recognized much sooner that the solution wasn't what was needed. True, the requirements document Jerry had been contracted for would have been abandoned or scaled back, but he surely wouldn't have been fired. He would have been part of solving the clarified problem.

Myth 2: You build trust by demonstrating competence

You wish that clients would trust you based on your technical competence. You have spent many years honing your technical skills. You take great pride in solving gnarly technical problems with aplomb. And it probably pains you to have to admit that all this glorious competence that you worked so hard for is completely invisible to most clients.

Client trust is not based on your technical competence, because clients usually aren't technical enough to appreciate it. Therefore, like it or not, they decide to trust you or not based on their experience of working with you.

Their experience is a proxy for your competence. You probably do the same thing whenever you're dealing with a professional whose specialty you're not familiar with. Imagine that you are going to engage a lawyer to write your will, yet you have no legal training. Would you be able to tell the difference between a good will and great will? And if I were to ask you whether your lawyer is any good or not, how would you judge?

You might think about things like:

* Did he answer my phone calls in a timely manner?

* Did he speak to me in language that I understood or in legal jargon?

* Was he condescending or rude?

* Did deliverables arrive on schedule?

* Was he forthcoming about delays, or did I have to follow up on missed deadlines?

* Did he charge me what he initially estimated?

Sound familiar? Yes, these aspects of your clients' experience are exactly the things they use to judge your technical competence. Fair or not, it's just how things work.

Their experience tells them whether or not you care. Have you ever desperately needed someone's help only to find they didn't seem to care at all about your problem? Say your flight was canceled and the counter agent seemed more interested in talking to her colleagues than getting you to your destination in time for a big meeting. You probably wanted to scream at her to move faster, but you knew that pissing her off wasn't a good idea, since you were completely at her mercy.

This is how clients often feel when working with contractors. They are completely dependent on us to get the technology they need to be successful and dubious about whether or not we care enough about them to do a good job.

But we often don't give our clients the sorts of signals that they rely on when deciding whether to trust someone. What kind of signals, you wonder?

Think back to that airline ticket agent. She sighs in resignation at your request. She doesn't acknowledge that you are in an urgent situation. She laughs at a co-worker's joke but won't look you in the eye. These are all cues that she doesn't care about you. When you are vulnerable, this is likely to make you combative, annoyed, and glad that your interaction with her will be over in five minutes.

In a professional environment, the cues might be slightly different, but no matter where you go, the difference between apathy and engagement is judged by whether or not you show signs of caring. Most clients have a great deal of experience with apathetic people. They may have even grown to expect apathy, detachment, and aloofness. But still they are on the lookout for cues that someone is really on their side. These cues include:

Feeling their pain – If you are unmoved by their pain and hold yourself so aloof from it that you send the message that it is not your problem, they will have less reason to trust you.

Shared enthusiasm – If you respond to their enthusiasm for the project without cracking a smile or sharing some level of excitement at the good results to come, they will have less reason to trust you.

Shared priorities – If you fail to resonate with what they consider most important about this project, you pass up a chance to confirm your personal commitment to the desired outcomes, and they will have less reason to trust you.

It has been said many times, and it bears repeating, that humans are not machines. Despite our love of clean, mechanistic systems, we should not expect humans to be mechanical. Language and physicality – faces, posture, and tone of voice – help us detect who is friend or foe. You need to reassure your client that you are friend, not foe. That's what building trust is all about.

8 WAYS TO ESTABLISH A STRONG RELATIONSHIP WITH NEW CLIENTS

1. Put yourself in your client's shoes

For clients, hiring a new consultant is something of an emotional roller coaster.

"As a client I am looking for someone I can trust," says David Maister. "The act of hiring a professional is, by very definition, an act of faith. I must, inevitably, believe a promise. In selecting a professional, I am not just buying a service; I am entering into a relationship."

When you think about it, how a new client feels is almost the polar opposite of how a newly hired consultant feels. It is a contrasting balance of hope and fear. Understanding these differences will help you to be more authentically empathetic.

Client 80% hope and 20% fear	Consultant 20% hope and 80% fear
I feel *vulnerable,* since I am taking a personal risk to trust this unknown person with my needs. I'm worried that he will make me look bad.	I feel respected and confident to be chosen to help with these needs. I have a great opportunity to enhance my reputation, learn new things, and get more business in the future.
I feel *out of control,* since I don't know enough about the consultant's specialty to judge how things are going.	I feel excited to solve these problems, since they're in my specialty. I feel *in control* of the domain of work allocated to me.
I feel *inadequate,* since I need help to complete the job I am responsible for.	I feel *smart,* since I'm being hired for my knowledge.
I feel *skeptical,* since I've been disappointed and even burned before by supposed experts.	I feel *trusted* to be selected and confident that I can deliver.
I am *cautiously optimistic* about all the benefits of the new technology and hope that it will solve my problems or open new opportunities.	I'm somewhat *worried that I can't deliver.* The technology may not be up to the task. I may not have the skills. The client may not give us the resources or support we need to succeed.

It takes extra work to empathize with someone who might be feeling the opposite of what you feel. But it is a necessary component of establishing relationships with new clients, who are in the midst of complex and conflicting emotions. It's especially difficult because their conflicting emotions are about you.

2. Find out what a real win looks like for your client

In order to earn your clients' trust, find out what their real goals are for your work. To do this, you need to know what their un-articulated goals are, and so do they. Then you can set about delivering a quick win, making sure that it benefits your client rather than you.

Remember Jerry? Great deliverables show how capable you are at following directions, but not how effective you are in helping make things better. If you want clients to know that you really care about delivering things that actually help them, your first step is to find out what's really important to them.

To do this, you need to ask some questions. This doesn't have to be some long, deep conversation. If your clients really do know what their goals are, these conversations go rather quickly. If they don't know, it will open a dialogue between the two of you that will lead to important answers for you both.

We recommend this process:

1. Tell your client that you want to get a better sense of the context for the project. Explain that doing so will help you make on-the-fly decisions down the line that support her goals.

2. Ask questions that get at the story behind the project.

    * Who will benefit most from this project?

    * What do you hope each stakeholder will say when it is done?

- What benefits will you personally experience when this is done well?

- Who could prevent this project from becoming a success? Why would they do so?

- Tell me the story of how this project was conceived and approved.

- Is this project solving a problem that is part of a larger problem?

- Finish this sentence for me: We will know we spent our money well when …

3. Using inductive reasoning, make inferences about what is most important about the project.

   - To the client personally

   - To the larger organization

4. Verify with the client your summary view of the project priorities, so that the client can agree, disagree, or elaborate.

Remember that there might be official priorities and unofficial priorities, and you have to keep track of them all.

3. Suggest changes to your deliverables if necessary

Once you get answers to questions about what will make your clients successful, evaluate whether what they explicitly asked for will really give them the best outcome possible. You need to decide what you believe will give them the best outcome based on:

- Your understanding of their goals

- A realistic assessment of their financial, technical, time, and political constraints

- Your knowledge of the technology
- Your assessment of your abilities
- Your assessment of their team's abilities

Usually, this exercise results in some minor tweaks to the job at hand. Occasionally, it may result in a project cancellation or a complete redesign of the work. Of course, there is a small risk that the client won't need your services once you point out that what was asked for isn't viable. But it rarely happens, and even when it does, the client usually finds another problem for you to tackle. There's no one more trustworthy than a consultant who is willing to make recommendations that are contrary to her own short-term self-interest.

Had Jerry done this, he would have quickly realized that the CFO was not going to support the solution he was being asked to write requirements for, and he could have suggested a more modest approach. Instead, he delivered a great document that turned out to be a loss for the CIO. The CIO looked bad in the eyes of the CFO for having proposed something that the CFO didn't want.

4. Show them your commitment

Showing your commitment to helping clients with what is most important to them is the best thing you can do to bolster the emotional aspect of clients' trust in you. This is not the same as having enthusiasm for solving technical problems, which most geeks have in abundance. This is not even the same as having enthusiasm for helping your client.

This is about expressing your desire to work with clients to address their deeply felt needs. They don't want to know that you are logically and dispassionately focused on doing a good job. They want to feel that your internal emotional state drives you to be helpful to them.

In fact, when we pick a team of people to do a project, one of the most important selection criteria we have is how much a person really wants to be on this project team. Frequently, we'll pick someone with more motivation to do the project over someone with more skills. The person with the motivation will get the skills, whereas the skilled person may not be motivated enough to apply his capabilities completely.

- How much do they want to build the product?

- How much do they want to play the role that I have for them?

- How much do they want to learn the technology?

- How much do they want to work with the other people on the team?

Notice how every question in that list involves the word "want." This is something that geeks often find uncomfortable because wanting is emotional. Wants are things geeks don't like to talk about or even admit that they have. They prefer to think dispassionately about objective reality. But desire can't be found in objective reality. You can't measure or prove its existence. Desire is inherently a felt experience, purely subjective. To communicate a subjective experience, you need to use words or body language.

No, we're not telling you to be someone other than who you are. Most geeks tend to be pretty low affect. They're not expressive like salespeople are. And you certainly don't want to try to falsely manufacture the outward signs of inner experiences. To do so would be inauthentic and easily detectable by most any human who can read face and voice cues. And this would undermine clients' trust in you.

If you agree that communicating your commitment is important, here's some advice to help you do it:

Feel it. The prerequisite to expressing desire is to actually feel it. And this can be foreign territory for many geeks. So our advice is to take three breaths while asking yourself, "How much do I really want to help this client?" And keep breathing until you feel a sense of certainty that, yes, you are committed to helping them with what's important to them. From that point on, what you say or do will be authentic and will be perceived that way.

Say it out loud. Give your client verbal cues to what's happening emotionally for you. You don't need to jump on the sofa and scream your head off to let people know what you're feeling. Just give it a name.

"I'm committed to …"

"I really want to …"

"I'm excited to have the opportunity to …"

The most important part of these sentences is the "I." In expressing commitment, you have to do it in the first person; otherwise it won't carry any emotional weight.

Let it show. Offer a reassuring smile, a nod of agreement, a handshake. All of these are cues of your commitment. If you are feeling committed, let it show in these ways. But don't put on a show of these things; just let them out, and know that they will have a good effect on building a relationship with your client.

5. Take responsibility in getting your point across

When you communicate, make sure you are understood. Too many technical people believe that just by saying something, they've communicated. They think that they can control the degree to which they are understood by controlling the clarity and precision of what they say. But what is clear and precise to geeks might be detail overload to someone with less technical knowledge.

There are a few things you need to do to ensure that your message has been received and understood.

Create a context for the information. Many clients can't process information without some sense of context, urgency, or responsibility for it. Most people need to be told why they should care before they can even begin to pay attention to information. Before you start rattling off technical details, make sure they know why it's important.

Focus on communicating what's important for them. Geeks, as a group, tend to believe in transparency, in sharing too much information rather than too little. But just because you can tell your client everything about your work doesn't mean that you should. Remember that their time and attention are scarce resources, so invest them wisely. Focus your communication with them on things that really matter to them as decision-makers and users of technology.

Make it safe to ask questions. A lot of clients don't like to ask geeks questions because they get confusing answers that often sound condescending. If they feel that asking you a question is going to result in useless information and a feeling of inadequacy, they're not going to bother asking. Let them know that you expect them to have questions, as this is not their specialty, and that you'll be happy to answer as best you can. Then take pains to explain things in a way that they can understand.

Observe and comment. Sometimes people don't even know what questions to ask. They know that they are confused, but don't have enough understanding to even formulate a coherent question. This makes them feel really bad. Watch for their expressions. When you notice furrowed brows, just say something like, "You look confused. Can I help?" They will then try to explain what they understood, and you get the chance to make sure that they got what you wanted them to get.

If you want to give new clients a good experience of working with you, you need to take responsibility both for what you say and for what they hear – you have to ensure that they got the message.

6. Tailor your message to the client

It's important to adapt your communication style and methods to the requirements of the situation. That includes accounting for the client's preferred approach and knowing whether that preference might change at different points in the project. Your job is to ensure that your approach is both effective and as comfortable as possible for your new client.

This includes accounting for:

Channel. Today, we have way too many choices in communication channels. You get to decide between face-to-face meetings, email, phone calls to fixed locations, calls to mobile phones, voicemail, instant messaging, text messages, Post-it notes on the monitor, and yes, even old-fashioned paper documents left on the seats of office chairs. Ask new clients how they prefer to receive information, but be sure that you also ask for multiple channels based on the urgency of the response you require.

Formality. Observe how people in the client organization communicate. Do they tend toward formal communication such as formatted memos and status reports and meetings scheduled long in advance with explicit agendas and presentations with PowerPoint? Or are they less formal, gathering people without notice or agenda to brainstorm on a project problem? In general, you should be able to adapt to their approach to formality. On occasion, it is valuable to use another method. For the informal group, you may want to use a formal document review to get their focused attention and build consensus around a particular topic.

Frequency. Ask your client how often they would like information about status, obstacles, and decisions. Although you should respect their desire for weekly, daily, or monthly information, you should also adapt the frequency to the urgency of the project and the specific requirements of the role you need them to play. Just because the client asks for monthly status reports doesn't mean you should wait an entire month for an urgent decision.

Change. It's also important to reassess your communication approach regularly throughout the project. If your client asks you to communicate via email but never responds, that doesn't relieve you of the responsibility for making your project successful. If what the client asked for isn't working, you need to shift to get what you need.

Also recognize that what works well may change over the course of the project. The slow turnaround of formal requirements documents via email may be fine during the initial phases of the project. But you may need to have standing daily meetings during the final, urgent push toward completion.

7. Demonstrate integrity

One of the most important things that new clients look for in consultants is integrity. Early on in the relationship, when clients feel most vulnerable, seemingly small things serve as cues for whether they can trust your integrity. Small transgressions become important symbols indicating to them that you can't be trusted on larger matters.

There are really only two rules, and no leeway in applying them. You must abide by them absolutely. The beginning of a new client relationship is not the time that you ask someone to cut you some slack. Rather than cutting you slack, they'll label you a slacker.

To feel confident that they can count on you, they want to know that:

When you say you'll do something, you'll do it. Even before you give them any quick-win deliverables, they will be looking for cues about you and your work, such as whether:

* You show up on time to meetings
* You send follow-up emails
* You keep track of open issues and follow up on them
* You are doing the activities you said you would

When you can't do what you said you'd do, you'll take responsibility for it. They feel that they can trust people who:

- Proactively inform them about missed deadlines and obstacles

- Explain what happened to prevent them from keeping their commitments without making excuses or shifting blame

- Acknowledge the impact on them of missing a commitment

- Commit to what they can do next to get things back on track

People with integrity get a chance to earn a position as go-to trusted advisors. People without it don't, no matter how technically talented they may be.

8. Deliver

Of course, you still need to deliver on the things that you've promised to do. For clients to feel comfortable that you can and will help them, you have to fulfill your promises. When you're delivering the right things to clients rather than the things that they asked for, their trust will grow and develop over time.

A FINAL NOTE

Once the client says yes, you've passed the basic test of being a plausible helper. The next move is yours. The quality and nature of the relationship you build with your new client is largely up to you. And the first impressions you make can result in anything from a long-term, productive, and profitable partnership to a short-term, contentious disaster.

The key to creating more positive relationships is to think carefully about new clients' first experiences of working with you, of how they feel, what they really need, and how you can earn the trust and respect that is the foundation of consulting relationships.

How you deal with these softer aspects of consulting will determine how much exciting technical work you get to do.

INTRODUCING NEW

TECHNOLOGY

TO CLIENTS

Here we have another of those key turning points in client relationships: first contact with technology. At the point of first contact, you've probably invested a lot of time and money in the development, customization, and deployment of the new technology. Whether the organization reaps the benefit of that investment depends on whether the technology gets used, and that's largely determined by that first-contact experience. In this chapter, we outline what you can do to get the best chance of a successful launch.

If you want to drive technology adoption in your organization, we've got a tough assignment for you. Go watch an old episode of *Star Trek: The Next Generation*, specifically Season 4, Episode 15, entitled "First Contact."

The *Enterprise* crew is assigned to a "first-contact" mission – to be the first aliens to make themselves known to the Malcorians, a race of humanoids on the verge of achieving warp speed space travel. The mission takes place after years of Federation reconnaissance, studying the culture and making plans to ensure that the introduction maximizes the probability of establishing good relations. Of course, even with all this preparation, things go terribly wrong, and the crew has to improvise. You'll just have to watch the episode to find out what happens.

The most important point here is that the Federation recognized the importance of the moment of first contact. It invested heavily in preparing for that encounter. It knew that it had only one chance to make a first impression and that careful planning was essential. In this, and in other sci-fi stories like it, the moment of first contact determines the trajectory of the interspecies relationship, and whether the contacted species becomes supportive allies or bitter enemies.

Similarly, in the moment that your users have first contact with a new technology, the course is set for whether or not they will adopt or resist it. If they have a good experience during that first encounter, there's an excellent chance that they will embrace your offering. If they have a bad experience, they will reject it, presuming that the technology will only bring them misery.

Unfortunately, folks in IT rarely pay much attention to what users experience when they encounter technology for the first time. All too often, the IT team is so overwhelmed with the logistics of deploying new technology that they don't even consider what the users' experience might be. They only think about the functionality. So they just push a new icon onto users' desktops and maybe email them a 500-page reference manual. After that, the users are on their own. IT just assumes that users will conduct a rational calculus of costs and benefits and logically adopt the superior new version. The IT folks expect the technology to speak for itself and for them.

But when you let technology speak for you, sometimes it says terrible things that you never intended – not about the technology, but about you. It is not uncommon for the hands-off approach to say the following things loud and clear:

* IT doesn't really know how important my job is.

* IT doesn't really care about helping me.

* IT cannot be trusted to give me usable technology.

Now, some of you might be saying, "Wait a minute, that's not fair! They shouldn't be judging me on how well I hold their hands. They should judge me on how good the technology is." That's not how they see it, though. For them, handholding is part of your job. And in fact, it just might be one of the most important aspects of your job.

Why? Because your technology is useless if it doesn't get used. And if users don't have a good experience using the technology, they won't use it. And if users don't use the technology, everyone suffers.

* Users don't get to realize the benefits of the new technology

* You become underappreciated, marginalized, and possibly outsourced.

So the stakes are high here. The success of your organization and the viability of your role in it depend on whether or not users adopt your technology. And, as we will see, your best hope of getting users to adopt new technology is to craft a positive experience for their first contact with it.

WHY MOST EFFORTS TO DRIVE ADOPTION FAIL

On the relatively rare occasions when IT people do try to drive technology adoption, the results tend to be disappointing, for three key reasons:

It's too late. Most efforts to drive adoption are started after the rollout is complete and users are already resisting the new systems. Unfortunately, these attempts are nearly doomed from the start. Fighting existing resistance is much harder than preventing it.

IT people are too focused on the technology. Too often, geeks think that the resistance is all about the technology. Even users fixate on the technology and usually explain their resistance in terms of some feature of the technology that they don't like. So the IT guys fixes whatever the user points at, thinking that he's solved the problem. But the truth is that users are rarely aware of why they really resist technology.

IT ignores the importance of the experience. Users' experiences are not the sum of the events that happen during the introduction. They are their interior emotional responses to those events. Their experience is not determined by the facts of what happened, but by their subjective reaction. So whether users resist or adopt technology is based on how they feel about it, how they feel about you, and even how they feel about themselves when they are using the technology.

If you focus your efforts on creating a good first experience for new users of your technology, they will be much more likely to embrace it.

HOW GEEK VALUES CONFLICT WITH CREATING GOOD EXPERIENCES

Two of the fundamental tenets of geek beliefs often get in the way of their giving users good first-contact experiences and ultimately undermine IT's ability to drive technology adoption.

Geeks believe that managing projects to key metrics results in success.

Focusing on traditional project management measures helps geeks to achieve important objectives within the project. They drive themselves to:

- Provide flawless technology

- Meet every deadline

- Come in under budget

- Include every feature users were expecting

And when geeks hit those goals, they feel great. They tend to think that meeting those objectives means they've won. But just because you feel good that you met your objectives doesn't mean that users will feel good about using your technology.

You can meet all of these goals and still create a completely awful experience for users. In fact, geeks do it all the time. Sometimes they get so single-mindedly focused on meeting these metrics that they lose sight of the human experience of those on the receiving end of their work. Ironically, their focus on these types of concrete metrics often inadvertently induces the resistance that undermines the adoption of the technology.

Geeks believe that their jobs are purely technical

Many IT people share a fundamental misperception about the responsibilities that come with their jobs. It may be that they tend to be a bit too literal about things in general. They tend to believe that if the title on their business card says programmer, their job is to write code, and if it says DBA, the job is to monitor and manage databases.

But every job in IT comes with an unstated, but essential, responsibility: to help organizations leverage technology. While programmers do this primarily by writing code and DBAs do this primarily by managing and monitoring databases, that's not the limit of what we owe our employers.

When geeks think of their jobs as simply providing technology that sponsors have requested, just as a vending machine would respond to four quarters at the press of a button, they fail to consider the human aspects of using the technology they create. They overlook the importance of providing the good first-contact experiences that their users need to successfully leverage the technology they give them.

What a good first-contact experience feels like

So if meeting your project management goals and giving users what they ask for doesn't create a good experience, then what does? It's not really that hard to understand. Pretty much everyone at work wants to feel:

Considered – People want to feel important enough to be thought about rather than overlooked.

Cared for – Not only do people want to be considered, but they want people at work to actually try to help them.

Empowered – People want to feel competent and in command of tools that help them do their jobs well.

Respected as learners – No one wants to be scoffed at when they are trying to learn something new.

Let's look at some examples of events that encourage and discourage these good feelings.

Feeling	Encourages	Discourages
Considered	Got early warning that the ERP upgrade was coming and explanation of how it would affect me.	New, unfamiliar version of ERP application showed up on my computer without warning, and now I don't know how to get my job done.
Cared for	The help desk person I talked to about the new application promised to call back in five minutes and did!	The help desk won't take calls. I have to submit a "ticket" through the website and then wait for god-knows-how-long until they call me. Until then, I can't do my job, and have no idea how long I have to wait.

Empowered	At the training for the new software, IT focused on the five operations I do every day and let me practice doing them in the new system. I feel confident I can hit the ground running, and I can see how the system will save me time and help me be more accurate.	IT sent me a confusing reference manual that looks like it was written for them to read. I can't even find how to do the two or three things I do most often. I did find directions for one thing, but I'm pretty frustrated after 20 minutes trying to figure it out.
Respected	When I called the help desk, they not only answered my question, but they explained how similar parts of the system worked. They were patient and eager to help me learn the new system.	When I called the help desk, the technician sounded annoyed that I had called and told me to look at a certain page in the manual to get what I needed. He asked me questions in a tone that sounded like he thinks I'm a three-year-old.

Of course, these are just a few extreme examples. To help create good experiences and drive technology adoption for your users, let's look at a simple process for creating a good first-contact experience.

HOW YOU CAN CREATE A GOOD FIRST CONTACT

Just as the Federation invested years of effort preparing for first contact with the Malcorians, you will need to make an investment in preparing for a good outcome for your users. Of course, you won't need years of work to do it. But the steps are similar.

- Understand where they are coming from

- Imagine what could go wrong

- Plan ahead to avoid disaster, promote good feeling

- Execute with kindness

Understand where they are coming from

There's no way you can create a good experience for your users if you don't know much about who they are and how they do their jobs. Remember that experience is an individual, subjective, emotional response to events. To predict how people will feel in a first-contact situation, consider things like:

- What's important to them about their jobs?

- How do they feel about using technology at work in general?

- How do they feel about your IT department?

- How are they likely to feel about the new technology you are giving them?

And as you answer these questions, you should keep in mind that not all resistance to technology is irrational.

1. Users have reasonable fears

Technology might be beautiful to you, but to most users, new technology at work is anything but benign. It signals a number of unpleasant possibilities.

Extra work. "I finally figured out how to use Version 2.0, and now I have to waste time figuring out how to use this Version 3.0."

Losing control. "This totally disrupts my routine. I won't be able to predict how long my work will take anymore. Once again, I will be at the mercy of those tech guys."

Feeling incompetent. "I hate it that I'm so bad with technology. It never makes sense to me, and I end up of having to ask all sorts of embarrassing questions. It seems to come so easily to other people, and I feel like such a moron."

Becoming obsolete. "If I don't learn this new system, my boss is going to think that I'm of no use anymore and fire me. Or worse yet, I might be replaced by a machine!"

2. Users have reasonable resentments

Users carry their past experiences with them, and they've all had experiences with technology and/or technical people that left them feeling bad. Fair or not, they come to your project with assumptions and biases that may have nothing to do with you, but can be quite powerful.

At one time or another they've all been confronted with:

* Condescending technical support people who treated them like idiots

* System bugs that prevented them from getting their work done

* Technical people who promised them something and then never followed up

* Reports with inaccurate information

* Confusing interfaces that left them feeling incompetent and bewildered

These types of experiences can leave people understandably leery of the process of adopting new technology.

Imagine what could go wrong

Once you have a good sense of who users are and how they think and feel, then you can get back to more familiar territory – risk management. If your job is to create a good experience for your users, then the next step is to consider the things that could go wrong. Your job here is to create a list of the things you can imagine happening that would trigger bad experiences

"Now wait a minute!" you might be saying. "Shouldn't we be coming up with ways to create a good experience?"

Well, yes. But we've noticed that it can be hard for geeks to come up with ideas about how to create an experience for another person. As problem-solvers, it's not our forte.

But we have found that when you ask a group of geeks how they might create an awful first-contact experience for their users, ideas fly out of their mouths faster than you can write them down. Have fun with it. A small group can have a real hoot brainstorming ways to really get users upset. Here are some quick examples of things that users would hate:

* Shut down the systems right before the user has a major deliverable.

* Deploy new systems without telling users.

* Make users work harder to accomplish the same tasks.

* Take away functionality that is critical to them.

* Display complete indifference to their distress.

- Take your own sweet time about following up on their urgent support request.

- Blame them and treat them like they're stupid when they can't figure things out.

- Don't answer the phone.

- Make them spend 15 minutes trying to log in.

- Give them data errors.

- Make sure they see a bug on the first three screens they look at.

- The people they contact for help are as lost as they are.

In just a few minutes, you can probably come up with a really good list like this that would capture experiences your users would hate. And the nice thing is that each item on this list is a problem that needs solving, and you can derive a very actionable list of things you need to do.

Plan ahead to avoid disasters, promote good feeling

Once you have your list of all the things you could do to create a good experience, it's time to decide which ones you should actually do. Then plan them into your project just like any other project task.

Given the unique situation of your users, the new technology, their history, their assumptions about technology, and their feelings about IT, you'll probably have some ideas that are specific to your situation. And that's as it should be.

Here, we're going to address the most common things you can do to create a good first-contact experience. In fact, these should apply to nearly every project you do.

Test the technology

Duh. Right? Of course everyone tests before deployment.

Of course it's important to test technology, but it's particularly important that the first few things that users see work well. The technology doesn't need to be perfect, but users need to experience a number of good things before they can absorb a bump in the road. If the first thing that they see when they click on that new icon is an error message, the first impression is settled, and it's not good.

Unfortunately, simple things often get overlooked. We have witnessed numerous cases where users were told that a new system or feature was in production and ready for them to use only for them to call back two minutes later to report a blank report or a button that did nothing after being clicked.

To technical people, these seem like minor oversights that take only a minute to fix. "Oops. I forgot to change the server name to the production server." Or, "Oh, the new screens are there. I just forgot to link the button."

But to users who are already feeling a bit skittish about trying out the new technology, these first impressions are a big deal. To you, these events probably seem inconsequential, carrying no inherent meaning, but to them it sets off major alarm bells. It signals things like, "This technology must be a sloppy piece of crap," and, "These IT people must be completely incompetent," and, "They must think I'm not important enough for them to check their work."

Court the influencers

Every work group has opinion leaders, people whom everyone respects. Whenever anything new or confusing comes up, everyone looks to the informal leaders to help decide if it's a good thing or not. And when that new technology shows up, everyone in the group will be looking toward those opinion leaders to help decide if they will embrace it or not.

One of the most overlooked opportunities to drive technology adoption is to include those user opinion leaders early and often. Invite them to be part of the project, testing technology and explaining priorities and operations. Most opinion leaders will be happy to be consulted, since this both recognizes and cements their position of respect. At the same time, it's good to show explicit appreciation for their support. They are busy people. A few words of thanks and some homemade brownies can go a long way.

Don't underestimate the power of a few encouraging words from these opinion leaders to their peers about the coming change. If they assure their co-workers that the new systems will be better for them and easy to learn, the team will most likely believe it and engage. If the opinion leaders say nothing or express skepticism, the team will likely resist.

Have a communication plan

Timing. Too often, we wait until a few days before deployment to dump overwhelming amounts of information on users all at once. We give them gargantuan reference manuals and hypnotically detailed training sessions and expect them to become immediately fluent with the new technology. And then we judge them for being ignorant when they look like deer in the headlights.

Imagine if an alien species suddenly appeared in your driveway, handed you an English-Alien dictionary and demanded that you immediately engage in peace talks right there in front of your house. You'd probably be left standing there motionless for hours as you processed just the fact of their existence. That's how users feel when we dump too much on them all at once.

Emotional content. Your communication plan needs to go beyond "just the facts." Referencing emotions will humanize the rollout. You might consider expressing:

* Excitement that the new software will bring many benefits

* Pride in how hard the team worked to meet the deadline

* Confidence that if problems arise the team will be able to solve them quickly

* Eagerness to hear feedback and to start in right away on optimizing

* Gratitude for the excellent input from business-side advisors and testers

* Assurances that support is easy to find and get

The day of first contact, users feel particularly fearful and vulnerable. So even if they don't end up needing extra support, it's important for them to see that it's available and that your team is ready to jump in to help them get started.

Make sure that all the users know exactly where to turn for immediate help. They should be able to reach a human being right away. Don't make them send an email into a black hole and wait for a response. They need to feel that they are not alone on that first day, so plan accordingly.

Have all hands on deck. Plan for getting as many people as possible focused on support for first contact. They should be visible to the users. If possible, deploy support people to locations where adoption of the software is critical. Having people physically present with the users sends a powerful message that you care about them and their productivity.

Provide business process support. If the new technology you are introducing is central to business processes (for example, invoicing, manufacturing, or sales processing), you'll need to ensure that both technical and business process support are available, because there will be questions about both.

Users only know that they're having trouble. They don't really distinguish between "I'm seeing an error message" and "I don't know how to enter an invoice anymore." Either way, they are feeling stressed, confused, and upset. Even though IT usually only provides technical support, make sure that you have partners in the business ready to help users with changes to their processes.

Practice kindness

Most technical support people think of their job as fixing technology and advising users. They think of it in factual, functional terms. Their job is to help people be productive.

But that attitude ignores the all-important experience that users have. They frequently hang up from help desk calls with their problems completely resolved, but their negative feelings completely unaddressed. The negative responses to the problem that led them to call still bother them.

A few words of kindness can transform a bad experience into a positive feeling of being cared for and helped.

So if your team isn't particularly skilled with social graces, take an hour and walk them through a few key phrases that will help them exhibit caring. This includes recognizing the inner experience of the users, and expressing their own inner desire to be helpful.

"I can see that this has been a frustrating situation for you. I'd like to help."

"I'd like to fix that as soon as possible"

"Thank you for finding that problem. It's important, and we missed it."

"I appreciate your patience, and I hope this hasn't interfered too much with your day."

"You've asked a lot of really good questions."

It may seem corny, but a little bit of practice saying kind words will make it easier for team members to find them when they are appropriate.

Execute thoughtfully and flexibly

After all that, you're ready to execute the first-contact plan. There are just a few key things to remember on the big day.

Display confidence and enthusiasm

One thing that's frequently forgotten is that in first contact, users pick up on the IT team's emotions, and that becomes a big influence on how they feel. If they see you looking fearful and skittish as they first encounter the technology, they will assume that there's something to be feared there. They resonate with your feelings.

On the positive side, if they see you looking confident and enthusiastic, they will resonate with that instead.

You don't want to be over-the-top, infomercial-crazy, phony happy. But you might be surprised how much your positive emotions affect their experience. Just point out a feature to a user and say something like, "Here's something I know you're going to really like," and watch what happens.

And if problems do occur, that's when they look to you most. If you display calm confidence in dealing with problems, they feel much better than if they see you panicking.

Acknowledge user feelings

During the flurry of activity during a first-contact day, it's easy to focus exclusively on handling technical issues. Of course, that should be the primary focus of the day, but not the exclusive one. As you work through the issues and interact with users, take a moment to acknowledge their feelings.

All it takes is something like, "I know that this is a bit frustrating, but we'll get this handled in just a few minutes." A few quick words convey a lot of positive information. It tells them that you care about them as human beings and not just about the technology. It tells them that they are important to you.

Remain flexible

And of course, remember that old saying, "No battle plan survives contact with the enemy." No matter how well you've planned, something unexpected will happen. Just stay calm, improvise, and work out the problems.

CONCLUSION

Don't resist change yourself. Embrace the idea that driving technology adoption is a key responsibility of the IT organization. All of your good technical work is of no value if no one uses it. Use your powers of analysis and problem-solving to craft a good first-contact experience for your users. If you just think about your users as an alien species, everything will be just fine.

RESTORING CLIENT TRUST

Here we have another critical moment in client or stakeholder relationships, a crisis of trust. Every geek leader at one time or another has to deal with clients who are unhappy. This chapter, excerpted from Paul's book 8 Steps to Restoring Client Trust, provides a clear and easily applicable process for restoring trust in a relationship.

Your client is unhappy, and you've got to do something. You've got a knot in the pit of your stomach. The stakes are high.

Maybe you're outraged and spoiling for a fight. Maybe you're stifling an urge to run from the room. Maybe you're on the verge of saying anything to appease the client and make this feeling go away.

This is when you need to keep your wits about you. You've got to find a way to handle the situation so that your relationship with the client is not damaged and trust is restored. If you handle the situation poorly, this client is history. And for most professionals, keeping clients is about more than money. It's a matter of personal pride.

If you recognize this situation, this book is for you. It will help you handle these tight spots powerfully and with integrity.

Believe it or not, if you handle the situation well, your client will be more loyal to you than ever. Clients who know that they can trust you to resolve tough situations are much more likely to keep working with you and to refer you to their friends.

In the 10 years since the first edition of this book was published, thousands of salespeople, lawyers, project managers, and technology professionals have used it to guide them through tough client situations. In fact, I have been amazed by the broad range of people who have written to me to share how useful it has been for them.

I originally wrote it for people like me, techno geeks, who find emotions at work baffling and frustrating. We just want rules to follow to help make sense of these intense situations. It turns out that all sorts of professionals find this approach useful, not just geeks.

Here are some rules for these tricky situations. I've broken them down into eight sequential steps that will give you your best chance at restoring your client's trust in you. You'll also find 20 tips for avoiding common pitfalls and preventing client unhappiness in the future.

So next time you've got an unhappy client, before you pick up the phone or hit send, pick up this book. Following these steps will help you form long, trusting relationships with your clients. Your career will thrive, and you'll sleep better at night.

UNHAPPY CLIENTS

As professionals, facing unhappy clients is one of the most difficult things that we do. Ordinarily, getting a call from a client is a pleasure. They want to seek our advice on issues of importance and to thank us for our valuable contributions to their businesses and lives. Sometimes they even want to buy more services.

No matter how competent, capable, and charismatic you are, at some point a client will be unhappy with you. You'll be surprised in a meeting. The phone will ring. Or you'll hear it through the grapevine. One of your clients is really upset with you.

How you handle that situation will determine whether you retain that relationship or lose the client.

Handling unhappy clients is particularly difficult for professionals. We identify with our work. It's an expression of self. We pride ourselves on its quality. When a client is unhappy with our work, we feel that he is unhappy with us personally, and we tend to feel threatened.

Customer service representatives for the phone company don't have this problem. For them, detachment is easy. They know that the irate caller isn't angry with them personally, just at the vague, distant monolith.

For professionals, irate clients threaten more than just personal comfort. They affect current and future financial stability by endangering the reputations that are built on happy clients. No single factor is more important to future sales.

Building a successful professional practice requires developing the skills to heal client relationships.

What makes clients unhappy?

Clients have high expectations regarding their professional relationships. When a client hires you, he has certain expectations about the results of your work together and the nature of your relationship. When you violate any of these, he may become disappointed, dissatisfied, or disillusioned.

Here's a short list of client expectations that are easy to violate. Generally, clients want:

- Respectful treatment
- Prompt responses
- Coherent explanations that they can understand
- Competent service
- Choices that they can make about their future
- Undivided attention
- Dedicated service
- Updates on progress and problems
- Confidence in your trustworthiness

And only lastly:

- Excellent technical work

As professionals, we are captivated by the quality of our work and often fool ourselves into believing that this is the most important thing to clients just because it's the most important thing to us. It's not. In fact, clients rarely know if your specialist, technical work is outstanding.

If a client knew enough about your specialty to distinguish outstanding technical work, he wouldn't need to hire you.

The cost of losing clients

It's been well documented that the cost of acquiring new clients greatly exceeds the cost of retaining clients. Selling work to someone who knows and trusts you is much easier than selling to someone who doesn't.

Why?

Simple. When selling professional services, you have only one thing to offer: *trust*. Think about it. Whether you're a consultant, lawyer, accountant, or other professional, the sales process is essentially the same. You discuss the client's problem and offer a service that will hopefully solve the customer's problem. Clients have to pay for services that they can't try out, sample, or review. They have nothing to go on but trust and hope.

Once you've worked with a client and he is satisfied, he is much more likely to trust you with more work rather than go out and try to find another professional who is completely unknown.

So once you've established a relationship, losing that client costs you a lot more than just the fees from that one project. For most professionals, repeat business is their bread and butter. When you lose a client, you lose:

* Future business from that client

* Business from those he would have referred to you

* Business from those he tells about his unhappiness

In short, the success of your career will be largely determined by your ability to handle client complaints.

The 8 steps

In this section, you will be introduced to the eight-step approach to productively resolve client conflict and restore trust.

1. Be prepared
2. Get the facts
3. Find the feelings
4. Let them know you got it
5. Dispute the facts (if you must)
6. Frame the problem
7. Handle the feelings
8. Handle the problem

Step 1: Be prepared

Usually, client unhappiness comes as a surprise. In fact, in my experience, it seems to show up most often when you are particularly proud of your work. Just when you think that the client will appreciate your brilliance, the client complains. There are occasional cases when you can anticipate some sort of concern, such as when you miss a delivery deadline or a project has run over budget. But, most of the time, you don't see it coming.

Your effectiveness at the moment of crisis will govern how difficult it will be to retain the client relationship. If you handle the first encounter poorly, it will be much more difficult to heal the relationship than if you handle it well.

That's why you need to be constantly prepared for client concerns. There are two ways to prepare:

Know the project and the environment. If you stay on top of the status of client projects, you will foresee many of the likely sources of dissatisfaction. Knowing what is going on in the rest of the client's environment also helps you anticipate problems. For example, if you are working on a marketing campaign with a customer and discover that one of the company's competitors has beaten it to the punch, you can expect the client to be frustrated and perhaps dissatisfied with the speed of the project.

Know the client culture. If the members of the client's organizational culture exhibit blaming behaviors, expect more problems. If the individual client you are serving has a negative outlook, steel yourself.

Prepare yourself

You must prepare yourself emotionally as well as intellectually for client conflict. If you have the luxury of a warning that the problem is coming, take a little time to put yourself in the right frame of mind to heal the relationship. Whatever your comfort level with conflict, it will help you to be prepared.

For those of you quite comfortable with confrontation (e.g., trial attorneys), it's important to realize that your clients may not be as comfortable as you are and you will need to prepare yourself to tone down your natural responses.

For those of you uncomfortable with confrontation, you need to steel yourself for some constructive conflict. It will drain lots of your energy, but avoiding it will only make things worse.

Most importantly, take some time to recognize your own emotions about the client, the project, and the individuals involved. Self-knowledge can be key to your ability to diffuse the situation. If you are unaware of your own feelings about the situation, you are much more likely to be drawn into an unproductive conflict in the heat of the moment.

Once you have a handle on your feelings about the situation, you must make a conscious decision to set your emotions aside – for the moment. If you are to repair the relationship, you must be able to put the client's feelings ahead of your own.

Care

The final thing you have to do in preparation for healing client relationships is to care about your client. Genuinely care.

Caring about clients requires sensitizing yourself to their problems and concerns, caring about their professional and personal well being, and committing yourself to the improvement of their condition. Although we all like to think that we care all the time, it's very easy to slip. It's very easy to lie to ourselves about the level of commitment to a client.

Caring for clients is *not*:

* Wanting their business

* Enjoying your fees

* Liking the challenging work they bring you

* Priding yourself on their prestige

These are ways of fooling yourself into thinking that you're concerned about them when you're really concerned about you.

Some professionals are good actors and think that they can fake it. I don't believe it. Simulated caring is not enough. We are pack animals, and at some level we can tell when someone's being disingenuous. If you can't really care about a particular client, you may want to consider:

* Not working with him

* Referring him to another professional

* Reducing his dependence on you

FIELD STORIES

Throughout this chapter we will follow the stories of two professionals and their experiences of client conflict: George, a project manager with a midsized IT consulting firm; and Janice, an independent communications trainer and consultant. These stories are composites based on real-world experiences.

GEORGE AND SANDY

George is an experienced project manager currently working with multiple projects at different client sites. At United Technologies, he is leading a group of programmers who are developing custom financial reports for Sandy, the chief financial officer.

Sandy has been with the company for eight years. She has a new boss, Roberto, the CEO, who has been with the company for only six months.

Joe is the lead programmer on the project. He is Sandy's day-to-day contact. Joe has successfully guided the project though half of the development of the software.

JANICE AND ED

Janice is an independent trainer and consultant focusing on interpersonal communications. She has been out on her own for 10 years. She presents her own custom courses at many large and small companies.

She has a two-year contract with Comcorp, a rapidly growing startup. Each month she delivers her introductory communications class to all Comcorp employees who have joined the company in the preceding month. Janice has delivered the monthly classes for 10 months. The student review forms at the end of each class have shown strong appreciation for the content and delivery of the course.

Ed, the new director of human resources, joined Comcorp six weeks ago. He has never managed a whole HR department before, and never worked in a startup.

STEP 2: GET THE FACTS

So you've prepared, but for what? The second step in repairing the relationship is getting the facts of the situation on the table. What's important here is to understand the facts *as the client sees them*. The purpose of this step is to get a clear picture of the client's beliefs about the situation – about what led up to and triggered the crisis.

Don't dispute the client's view of the world at this time. You may not agree that the client's facts are indeed facts. That's not important now. You're not trying to establish objective truth. You're just trying to learn what the client believes. There will be plenty of time later to come to agreement about what really happened and what it meant.

The key goal of this step is to understand, not to fix. If you don't understand what led to the breakdown in the relationship from the client's point of view, you have no hope of addressing the issue and saving the relationship. In other words, you can't fix what you don't see.

The key skill for success in this step is listening. You must be able to set aside your own feelings for the moment and listen to:

- What the client says

- What the client doesn't say

- What the client doesn't know how to say

Each will give you important insights into how to handle your situation.

Listen to what the client says

The first thing that you must listen for is what the client is actually saying. This will give you the first clues to the situation and the triggers for your client's unhappiness. You will get a good picture of his immediate concerns and the level of urgency that the client places on the problem.

Focus your best listening skills on the client. Hearing what other people say – really hearing them – is very difficult. We spend most of our educational lives learning to think clearly and express ourselves articulately, but we are never taught to listen effectively.

Listening carefully to someone who is upset with you is especially difficult. It is a process with numerous barriers that you must be aware of and careful to avoid. Most of the time when others are talking we are:

- Thinking about what to say next

- Waiting to talk

- Filling in silently what we think is being said

- Daydreaming, not paying attention

- Anticipating what we think is coming next

At this moment in the process of restoring trust, it is critical that you avoid these traps. You must focus on what the client tells you and then clarify it with him. To do this you should:

- Ask open-ended questions (ones that can't be answered yes/no)
- Listen to the responses
- Ask clarifying questions
- Paraphrase what was said to ensure that you got it.

Listen to what the client doesn't say

Once you've clearly understood what the client has to say, keep listening. In fact, while you are listening to what he is saying, you also have the opportunity to listen to what he is *not* saying.

Although understanding what the client tells you is important, it may be more important to recognize what he is UNWILLING to tell you. Those hidden thoughts generally hold more power than those things that a client will tell you. They are the ideas that he has thought about enough to make a conscious decision not to share.

Unspoken thoughts offer your best glimpse into the emotional content behind the unhappiness. This may seem like an oxymoron.

How can you listen to what's not said? Easy. Listen for things like:

- Aborted sentences
- Long pauses
- Avoided subjects
- Unanswered questions

When any one of these things happens in the conversation, the client has probably decided to conceal something. At those times, you can often fill in the blanks and guess what's on the client's mind.

Making an educated guess about what's on the client's mind after listening to what the client says and doesn't say is not the same as making assumptions before listening. It's important to hear completely before adding your own interpretation.

Listen to what the client doesn't know how to say

Finally, you need to listen for those things that the client doesn't know how to articulate. As with listening for what's not said, this too requires advanced listening skills. You must be able to analyze both what's said and what's not to determine whether something's missing. When they don't add up, there is often some unspoken concern that lies at the heart of the matter.

In the heat of confrontation, client complaints sometimes seem petty or small. Clients complain about things that ordinarily would be minor annoyances, yet the emotional force behind their concerns seems disproportionate to the magnitude of the complaint.

This is one key tip-off that the client is unable to translate real concerns into words – that whether or not he is willing to share his real issues, he cannot. The upsetting image is locked away, blocked by emotion, lack of clarity, or inadequate vocabulary.

When you listen very carefully to the words that a client uses in describing the situation, he will give you clues to the hidden concern. The subtle shades of tone will guide you toward understanding the nature of the problem.

SANDY TELLS GEORGE SHE WANTS JOE GONE

At 2:30 on Friday afternoon, George picked up his voicemail messages and was disturbed to hear one from Sandy time-stamped at 12:30. In a rather agitated voice, she said, "George, where are you? I need to talk to you right away. I want Joe out of here, and we need to have a replacement in by Monday morning."

George's first thought was that there was no one else available who could do the job. And even if there were, it would be a terrible idea to remove the only person with a complete technical understanding of the system midway through the project.

But he knew that his facts would have to wait.

First, he needed Sandy's facts. George took a deep breath and dialed Sandy's number. "Sandy? George. I got your message. What happened?"

"George, I've had it with Joe. I want him out of here today."

"What happened?"

"And I'm not going to pay for the last two weeks either."

"Sandy, what happened?"

"This is the second Friday in a row that I can't find Joe. I didn't get my status report and have no idea how things are going." Sandy stopped.

George waited silently until Sandy finally added, "I went to a meeting with Roberto and I got blindsided."

ED ACCUSES JANICE OF UNETHICAL BEHAVIOR

Janice was in her home office, having spent a quiet morning catching up reading the backlog of journals and magazines piled up in her office. When the phone rang, she was startled by the sudden break in the silence.

"Janice, this is Ed, the new HR director at Comcorp, and I need to talk to you about the false charges on your most recent invoice."

Janice was quite taken aback. Not only had they never spoken before, but in 10 years of consulting, no one had ever accused her of falsifying an invoice. She prided herself on her integrity, and this sort of attack was like waving a red flag in front of a bull. She took a deep breath.

She knew immediately what he was referring to. There was a special charge for a canceled class that she and Ed's predecessor had agreed to verbally.

"Are you referring to the canceled-class fee?"

"Yes, and your contract states that there will be no cancellation fees. I don't work that way. Your services will no longer be required."

"Ed, I hope that you don't take this the wrong way, but I'm concerned that you haven't asked me why that's there. Would you like to know, or do you just want to cancel the contract?"

STEP 3: FIND THE FEELINGS ABOUT THE SITUATION

When a client complains to you, there are two distinct things that he is trying to communicate.

* His view of the facts surrounding and triggering his dissatisfaction

* His feelings about those facts

Only rarely will a client explicitly point out his emotions, but the whole reason that you're having the conversation is emotional. Dissatisfaction is an emotion, not a fact.

So just sticking to the facts is unlikely to heal the relationship. You need to deal with both the reasons and the reactions. There are several ways you can discover what your client is feeling.

Watch and listen. The more emotionally charged the situation, the easier it will be to figure out. If the client's face is red, his veins are bulging, and he is screaming at you, there's a good chance that he's angry.

Make a statement about the emotions, and then shut up. If given an opening, many clients will tell you what they are feeling. Give them the chance by saying something like, "You seem very frustrated." Then don't say anything. Allow the client to fill the silence. He will often tell you what's going on for him.

Ask. Although it feels odd to some people, you can ask what someone is feeling in a work setting. When a client gives you a fact about the problem, just ask, "How do you feel about that?" Often, they'll tell you.

GEORGE SHOWS SANDY EMPATHY,
GETS A FULLER PICTURE

George was starting to get the picture. Sandy was probably embarrassed and angry. George continued with questions.

"What did Roberto hit you with?"

"He wanted to make a decision about whether to expand the project to include another set of reports, but only if the current scope was under control. He had run into Joe in the hall a few days ago and got an update. He knew more about my project than I did!"

George waited a moment and then quietly said, "That must have been an embarrassing position to be in."

Sandy blurted out, "You bet it was. I felt like a total idiot. He probably thinks that I can't manage anything. And Roberto is still relatively new here. I can't afford that sort of exposure. I need someone in here who's going to help me, not someone who's going to make me look like a moron."

George asked, "Is there anything else here that I should know about?"

Sandy paused and then added, "Even when Joe does give me information, it's usually not in a form that makes sense. He doesn't understand what I need."

George could feel the pent-up frustration and surmised that Joe's technical explanations probably made her feel incompetent.

JANICE STANDS UP FOR HERSELF, WHILE AFFIRMING ED'S FEELINGS

Now Ed was taken aback. "Excuse me?" he managed to spit out.

"Ed, I'm not used to being accused of defrauding my clients, and you are calling me with what seems like some awful assumptions about my ethics that you clearly have some strong feelings about."

"I've only been here six weeks, and I've been finding contractors robbing this place blind everywhere I look."

"If that's true, I can understand your outrage, but it doesn't seem fair for me to be presumed guilty and lumped in with a bunch of con artists. I imagine that you're probably under a lot of pressure to show quick results."

"My mandate is to transform this department into a professional HR organization within six months, and I'm starting by tossing out the deadwood."

"Ed, it sounds like you've got a real challenge. It sounds intimidating, almost overwhelming. I'd like to clear up this invoice issue and sit down with you to share my observations of the department over the last year. When can we get together?"

Step 4: Let the client know you get it

Now you begin to address the relationship problems. The other steps have laid the foundation for the resolution, but this is the turning point. Until this point, you have been gathering information from the client without challenging, defending, or questioning.

Once you have uncovered both the client's view of the facts of the situation and his feelings about it, it's time to make sure that the client understands that get it. This is critical because:

* It diffuses some of the emotion

* It shows respect

* It ensures that the client knows that you're both trying to solve the same problem

You do this by:

* Summarizing what you've learned about the facts and emotions

* Asking the client if you've got it right

If the client says yes, then move on to the next steps. If the client says no, or offers clarifications, go back to Step 2, and continue doing this until the client agrees that you get it.

Once the client agrees that you understand his facts and feelings, you've created common ground. You now have created a common reality from which you can begin to heal the relationship.

GEORGE RESTATES WHAT HE HEARD SANDY SAY

George felt that he had the information that he needed and that it was time that Sandy should know that he was listening.

"Sandy, I'd like to take a moment to recap to make sure that I've understood what's going on here. Is that okay with you?"

"Okay, go ahead."

"I would appreciate it if you would stop me if I've got something wrong, because I want to be sure that I understand. What I heard was that you are feeling frustrated with Joe for two reasons, one immediate and the other longer term. The immediate reason is that you haven't been able to find Joe to get status updates on the last two Fridays and that led you to be embarrassingly blindsided in a meeting with Roberto. The longer-term frustration that I heard was that even when you do get information from Joe, it's not always in a form that makes sense to you. Would you say that that is an accurate summary of the situation?"

"Yeah. That's pretty much it."

"Okay. Thanks. I think that I understand."

JANICE CONFIRMS SHE HEARD
WHAT WAS IMPORTANT TO ED

The following week, Janice and Ed met in his office at Comcorp.

Janice started out, "I appreciate your time, and I hope that we can clear the air today. I'd like to talk to you about two things. I'd like to confirm what I have heard already and learn more about what I haven't yet heard. I'd like to start out by making sure that I heard you clearly in our last conversation. Is that okay with you?"

"Go," Ed said succinctly.

"First, I understand that you have a concern over the validity of a class-cancellation fee on my last invoice that was not specifically called out in our contract. Second, because of the charge, you would like to cancel our two-year contract. Correct?"

"So far, you've got it right."

"I also heard that you've got a mandate to transform this department in six months and that you are starting out by eliminating questionable contractors."

"Yup."

"That's what I heard, but what I didn't hear was whether you have any other concerns about my services beyond the invoice. Are there any other problems?"

"Well, since you asked, I talked with two new employees, and neither liked your class much. I can't afford bad training."

STEP 5: QUESTION FACTS (IF YOU MUST)

Now that you've gained agreement from the client that you've clearly heard his facts and feelings, you have a big decision to make: whether to dispute the client's version of the facts.

You cannot question clients' feelings. Their feelings are theirs and are not subject to question. Not only would that be pointless; it would be deeply disrespectful and insulting as well. Clearly it's not a productive thing to do.

However, from listening carefully to the client, you have earned the right to question his version of the facts.

This is a very dangerous thing to do at this point. The relationship has only begun to heal, and you may disrupt the progress by questioning the client's reality. Unless he has a VERY IMPORTANT fact wrong, it's probably not worth it.

If you disagree with the client's interpretation of the facts rather than the facts themselves, do not bring it up now. That's what the next step is for.

It can be very difficult to disagree with a client's facts and refrain from correcting them. You must keep your need to be right under control. It will not serve your goal of retaining the client relationship.

If you must disagree, do so politely and carefully. It may be best to ask for time to investigate the situation, and then get back to the client shortly to continue the conversation.

GEORGE TELLS SANDY WHERE JOE WAS

"Sandy, I can understand your frustration, but there is one thing that I think we need to discuss. Last week, on Wednesday, you and I discussed briefly that I needed Joe for one day to help me out on another project. I know we didn't have an extended conversation about it, but I did clear it with you. That said, you still should have received a status update regardless of whether Joe was there on Friday or not. Do you remember our discussion about last Friday?"

"I suppose I do," Sandy said slowly. "But that doesn't change my mind about wanting Joe out of here."

"I understand. I just want to make sure that we're on the same page and that Joe isn't being blamed for more than he is actually responsible for. Does that seem fair to you?"

"I suppose so."

"Now, the reason you couldn't find Joe this morning is that he had a dentist appointment. He told me about it last week and I thought he had told you also. So on this, I have to apologize, because it's my fault you didn't hear about it. I need to be clearer with Joe about sharing scheduling information with you as well as me."

JANICE TELLS ED ABOUT AN AGREEMENT
WITH HIS PREDECESSOR

Janice continued, "Anything else?"

Ed answered, "No, that's it. That's why I want to cancel."

"Well, given the picture you must have of me and my services, I can understand your position. I'd like to start with the class-cancellation fee. This was a special, one-time charge that your predecessor and I agreed to when he canceled a class after I had already traveled to your Cambridge offices. He knew that he was going to cancel a week in advance and forgot to tell me. Not only did I incur all the travel expenses and lost time, but I also turned away another client for that week. We agreed that it would be fair that Comcorp at least pay for my travel expenses. That's what is contained in that charge. You can check with Connie in Cambridge if you'd like to confirm this."

"Okay, I'm not sure that I agree with the decision, but I will live with it," Ed offered.

"I have also brought along the complete class review forms for all 10 of the classes that have been completed. Although the two people you talked to may not have been thrilled, I don't think that they represent a good sample. You'll find that the average scores are 4.5 out of 5 for student satisfaction."

STEP 6: FRAME THE PROBLEM

Once you and the client have agreed on the facts and feelings of the situation, it's time to jointly agree to the meaning. That meaning is the frame in which we place the facts. We often like to pretend that there is only one true interpretation of a set of facts, but it's not true.

Every set of facts can have multiple frames. For example, imagine that you and I are working together on a project and we agree that it is behind schedule. You may frame the situation such that it means that I am a slow worker. I may frame the situation such that we underestimated the effort required. Both of the meanings are validly constructed from the same facts.

In order to resolve the problem, you have to agree with the client what the actual problem is and about how to frame the situation. Since the client is upset, we can assume that the client has already framed the situation, and it is a frame that reflects poorly on the service provider.

Assuming that you want to continue to try to heal the relationship, you have two choices. You can accept the client's frame and offer restitution, or you can reframe the situation. There are times when it is appropriate to accept the client's interpretation, but most situations require reframing.

Proactively framing the situation requires taking much more control over the meaning of the situation than you have up to this time. Should you decide not to reframe the situation, skip to the next step.

Identify the client's mental model

The first step in reframing the situation is to identify the mental model that the client is currently applying to the situation.

A mental model is a simplified version of reality that we use to interpret a situation. Some models take the form of images or analogies that we use to reason about a situation (e.g., "This problem is like a boat going over a waterfall, and we're in the boat"). Other models take the form of rules and assumptions (e.g., "If we encounter turbulence during our airplane flight, the plane might crash").

So a client's mental model is a set of images, assumptions, and/or rules that govern his thinking about the situation. You've already uncovered much of the information about his assumptions and about the facts and feelings that he has. Adding your observations about the language used to describe the situation will often give you a clear idea of the client's mental picture of the problem.

For example, imagine a situation in which a client is upset by being surprised that a project you are working on together is late. He may have a mental picture of you deliberately hiding information from him in order to be self-serving and manipulative. You might figure this out from statements like, "Consultants always hide bad news."

Once you've figured out the mental model that the client is applying, you will also probably have a very good understanding of why he is upset.

Create your own mental model

Now you must create your own model of the situation to replace the client's. Your model must not only be consistent with the facts that you've agreed to, but also be a more compelling interpretation of the facts than the one that the client has already adopted.

Finding an appropriate model is often a very intuitive exercise. However, here are two categories of models to help you generate ideas for your own interpretation.

Case-based models. Some models are built by extrapolating from one or more examples of situations. They are constructed by making inferences about general rules based on specific cases. These case-based models tend to be built on a limited number of experiences from which we infer general rules based on similarities of the cases (e.g., rule: lawyers always charge more than they say they will; cases: both times I've gone to a lawyer, the bill has been higher in the end than the estimate at the beginning).

Rule-based models. Rule-based models are exactly the opposite of case-based models. Rule-based models are based on abstract concepts and then tested against specific cases to check whether the rules deduced hold against reality. They can be deeply held beliefs that we are taught as children (e.g., rule: if you put your elbows on the dinner table, you are being rude). They can also reflect moral or ethical principles (e.g., rule: eating animals is wrong).

You can use either to develop your mental picture of the client situation.

Communicate the model

No matter how compelling your alternative model of the situation is, if you do not communicate it to the client powerfully, you will be ineffective at changing the client's mental model.

You must deliver the new interpretation in such a way that the client not only understands it, but also finds it convincing enough to abandon previously held ideas.

In their book, *The Art of Framing*, Gail Fairhurst and Robert Sarr identify five different ways to forcefully communicate mental models.

Metaphors efficiently deliver imagery and analogies. They are used to show how the current situation is like something else (e.g., "We've been approaching this problem with a shotgun rather than a rifle").

Jargon places a set of facts in familiar terms. It can create a set of strong associations with a very small amount of language.

Contrast shows how a situation is unlike another. It describes things by their opposites. Often it's easier to describe things by what they're not rather than by what they are.

Spin is less an attempt to change the meaning of a situation than it is an attempt to change the value judgment of it. It's really an attempt to influence whether the situation is viewed as good or bad.

Stories frame situations by example. They appeal especially well to people who tend to prefer the case-based models.

You need to select the approach to communicating the frame that will resonate best with this particular client.

GEORGE REFRAMES JOE'S ROLE

George realized that they had reached a critical point in the discussion. They had agreed on the facts of the situation and now had to come to an agreement on the meaning of the facts.

He understood that Sandy's mental model was driving her unhappiness with Joe. She felt that Joe was inattentive to her needs and secretive about his work habits and the progress of the project. She thought that this sort of attitude would likely result in further problems as the project progressed.

George felt that the project itself was progressing well and that a change to the staffing of the project at this moment would jeopardize not only the project but also the customer relationship.

Also, George realized that although he had addressed most of Sandy's factual complaints about Joe, her emotions remained unchanged.

"Sandy, I think the failing in this situation has been mine and not Joe's. He's a young technical guy and I've been relying on him too much to keep you informed. He's been working very hard to keep this project on track, and I think he's done a good job of it. From a technical standpoint, the project is progressing well. Clearly, I need to do a better job of working with you. I think it would be a mistake to remove Joe now."

JANICE SEES THAT ED FEELS TRAPPED

Ed agreed to look over the student reviews, but Janice felt that Ed still wasn't satisfied. Although he had not directly said so, she believed that Ed felt trapped by the long-term contract and that it prevented him from making visible changes to the department's projected image.

Ed's mental model was that of a trapped animal looking for any way out of a cage. She might have blocked his immediate objections (escape attempt), but he wasn't done yet. Janice realized that she needed to change Ed's image of her from jailer to partner.

"Ed, I'm not in the business of trapping my clients. I'm in the business of helping them. We entered into a long-term arrangement to reserve dates and reduce costs. If after our discussion today you still want out, I'll be happy to discuss cancellation. But before we do that, I'd like to talk about how we can change what we do together to help your mission of transforming the department. Do you have a vision for the role you want training to play in the department?"

"Not specifically. I haven't had a chance to really dig into it. I've been so busy fighting fires and cleaning up messes."

"Do you have a plan for how you're going to develop that vision?"

"Not yet."

STEP 7: HANDLE THE FEELINGS ABOUT THE PROBLEM

By this time you and the client have built a consensus about the facts, feelings, and frames of the situation. Finally you are prepared to resolve the problem in a manner that will allow you to continue the relationship.

First, you must handle the feelings about the problem. Handling feelings doesn't mean that you can fix them. You can only try to get past them.

There are several generic approaches to handling the client's feelings:

Empathize – Sometimes a little understanding is all that's required. There may be nothing specific that you can do about the client's hurt feelings other than to let him know that you understand how he feels (e.g., "I understand how this must make you feel").

Apologize – If it's appropriate, you may apologize for either the facts or the feelings (e.g., "I'm very sorry that this happened," or, "Even though the problem was unavoidable, I'm very sorry for the stress that this has caused you").

Ask what to do. Sometimes it's not really clear that there's anything concrete that you can do about the client's feelings. In those cases, it might be best to ask the client something like, "What can I do to make this less painful for you?"

Be honest about your feelings related to the problem. If you have feelings about the situation that are appropriate to share, this is the time to do it (e.g., "I'm so frustrated by this").

GEORGE SHOWS SANDY THAT HE UNDERSTANDS HER FEELINGS AND APOLOGIZES

George continued, "Don't punish Joe for my mistakes. I can't tell you how sorry I am to have caused you embarrassment in front of Roberto. I feel terrible about it. I'm sure you know that it was unintentional, but that probably doesn't make it any easier to accept. Is there anything I can do to help restore your relationship with Roberto?"

"No. I don't think there's any permanent damage, but I can't afford for that to happen again." Sandy seemed to be calming down a bit but was still clearly agitated.

"I understand. If you can accept my apology, I'd like to talk to you about what we can do together to ensure that this doesn't happen again."

"Well, what do you propose?"

JANICE PROPOSES TO HELP ED WITH
THE POLITICS OF THE SITUATION

"Ed, I can share with you what happened last time we tried to design a training program here. It turned out to be much more of a political minefield than we anticipated. The operations and the research department heads have very different ideas about what sort of training their people need. But the CEO insists that we have the same program for everyone. If you would like, I can pull my notes and review them with you. Then we can work together to design an approach to building a consensus with the department heads. Would that be helpful?"

"I suppose that it would. I hadn't really planned on involving them in the process until we had a training approach in place. Now that you mention it, your idea sounds less risky. What would it cost?"

"I don't know yet. I'll put together some options for you for the next time we meet. That way, you can choose how much or how little you would like me involved. Are you comfortable with that?"

"That sounds fine."

Janice sensed that Ed's stern mood was lightening a bit.

STEP 8: HANDLE THE PROBLEM

Finally, you are ready to deal with the substance of the problem.

This is the part that you as a professional have trained your whole career for. Most professional work is structured around finding problems and solving them through the application of the techniques of a specific discipline.

Computer programmers write software to solve problems. Architects design buildings and spaces to solve problems and meet needs.

Based on the facts of the situation that you and the client have agreed to, you will construct an appropriate plan to restore the work or relationship to health.

Depending on the nature of the breakdown, there may be many remedies, including financial exchanges, personnel changes, or unpaid work. There may be none.

Whatever you and the client agree to do together to restore the relationship to health, I recommend two specific things.

Document the agreement. Write a short letter that captures the essential elements of the conversation. It should describe what you and the client agree are the relevant facts and frame. It should also include any remedial actions to be taken. And while it may contain information about feelings, this will be relatively rare.

Follow through. No matter what you agree to, it is imperative that you follow through on your promises. If you do not, there is little hope of restoring the relationship.

If you follow these steps in order, you have a good chance of healing your client relationship.

GEORGE SUGGESTS TWO CONCRETE SOLUTIONS

"There are two things I can think of immediately that should help the situation. First, I need to get Joe a company cell phone right away. That way, even if he's not at his desk, you should be able to find him more easily. Second, I'd like to schedule a regular weekly meeting with you so that the two of us can calibrate on the progress and problems related to the project in a more formal manner. After a few weeks I think we should review the frequency of this meeting in order to strike a balance so that you are comfortable with the amount and timeliness of information, and that I'm not wasting your time. I would hate for you to feel that you're not getting what you need. At the same time I'd hate for you to dread every time I walk into your office. How does that sound to you?"

"I think that would be a good start. We should try it out and see how it's going in a few weeks."

"Sandy, I appreciate your willingness to work with me on this. Again, I'm really sorry that this happened, but I'm confident that within a few weeks you'll be comfortable with our progress. When would you like to schedule our first meeting?"

JANICE SETS A TIME FOR STRATEGIC REVIEW

Janice saw that their half-hour was almost up. "I notice that we are almost at the end of our scheduled half-hour, and I don't want to put you off schedule, so I'd like to suggest that we return to the two immediate issues that brought us here. Are you comfortable with the one-time cancellation fee?"

"Yes, I understand it and will approve the bill for payment. But I don't want to continue with the classes that you have been teaching."

"That's fine. What I would like to suggest is that we put next month's class on hold and use the time for the strategic review that we will discuss at our next meeting. After that review, then we'll have a clearer idea of what sort of training would serve your needs."

"That sounds good. What would that mean for our costs?"

"That will depend on the options that you choose at our next meeting. Once you make that selection, we'll know whether we can continue to work together, or we will discuss cancellation. It'll be up to you. Sound fair?"

"Yes. I'm comfortable with that. Thanks for coming in, Janice."

CONCLUSION

Let's face it: Client conflict feels bad – really bad. At these moments of crisis, it's essential that you focus less on yourself and more on your client and her feelings. And you need to be prepared to handle it immediately, openly, and productively. You don't get a do-over with these situations.

As you become more adept at restoring client trust, you will start to recognize these painful episodes as the opportunities that they are. When you successfully navigate a rough patch with your clients, they will trust you even more. It's one thing to trust someone who has never let you down. But there's a much deeper connection that's reserved for people with whom we have shared hard times. Of all the turning points in stakeholder relationships, this is the one that has the greatest potential to make or break your projects and, frankly, your career.

A GEEK'S GUIDE TO PRESENTING TO BUSINESS PEOPLE

As a leader, it is your job to influence people outside of your team to take actions that benefit your team and the organization as a whole. We have devoted this chapter to one of the most mysterious aspects of geek leadership, the question of how to move business people to act. We also think that the nuances of delivering great presentations to business people are transferrable to other situations when you find yourself needing to change someone's mind.

A lot of people consider public speaking to be one of life's most stressful events. And for geeks, presenting to business people is especially terrifying. Business people – the term geeks use to refer to everyone who isn't technical – often seem confusing and capricious to geeks. They often respond badly to the way geeks like to present things. So, it's not surprising that many geeks shy away from giving presentations to such unpredictable people.

But you can avoid it for only so long – if you want to get anything done. In fact, if you want to grow in your career, you're going to have to present to business people, and do it well. In the future, successful geeks will be the ones who can bridge the divide between technical and business groups. And presenting to business people is a critical part of working across these disparate cultures.

Luckily, it's not really that hard if you prepare properly. You don't need to be a charismatic speaker to be compelling and effective. You just need to be relevant and focused, and that happens as a result of your preparation.

If you invest in preparation, not only will you accomplish your goals, but you'll also find that giving presentations isn't all that difficult. You won't experience the sort of fear and trepidation that most people do. You'll feel empowered to get up in front of a room and be yourself. And all it takes is for you to follow this simple, five-step process:

1. Clarify your goal
2. Get into their heads
3. Craft a transformation (write it)
4. Present, connect, and resonate
5. Conclude with a call to action

CLARIFY YOUR GOAL

As geeks, we organize our thinking around problems and solutions, and that's a powerful framework for presentations. Start out by thinking carefully about what problem this presentation is intended to solve. What do you want to see changed as a result of this presentation? In other words, what will be transformed by this event?

Imagine that you've been asked to lead a team that will recommend a new CRM package to your company. You've assembled the team, and the project sponsors have asked you to present your approach before investing a lot of time in execution. What do you want to be different after the meeting? Do you want them to give you their blessing to proceed? Do you want them to feel comfortable that you've got things under control? Do you want them to abandon the project completely?

If you can't clearly state what you want to accomplish, postpone the event until you can, or cancel it altogether. If someone asked you to present and it's not obvious what it will accomplish, go to her and get the answer. If she can't answer it, cancel the presentation. We're serious. This is really fundamental. It's like developing code before you have any idea about what the requirements are.

That said, the most common purposes for presentations to business people are to:

Influence decisions – You want a decision-maker to make a choice that you think is best, or at least for her to understand the trade-offs.

Manage expectations and share status – You want people to be aware of what's going on with something so their expectations are in line with reality. Usually it's a project you're working on.

Leverage opportunities – You want people to focus attention on something you consider important. Usually this involves sharing information about what's going on in the industry or with a project.

Leverage technology – You want a user to be able to use some sort of technology effectively.

How you structure your material will depend on what you're trying to accomplish and who the audience is. And when you start with the problem you're trying to solve with the presentation, it will give you essential insight about what to say and how to organize it.

GET INTO THEIR HEADS

It's time to turn your attention to the audience. Since you're thinking about the presentation as a transformational event, as somehow changing the current state of the situation into one in which your goals are met, you have to think about what the audience members need in order to change. Understanding what they need requires answering three questions:

- What's their starting point?
- What do they really need to know?
- What do they need to feel?

What's their starting point?

Begin by identifying obstacles. What about the current state of the audience prevents your goal from already being met? Here are some questions to ask yourself about your audience:

- Are they missing information that you have?
- Do they have priorities that are different from yours?
- Are they attached to a particular course of action? Why?

- Are they in some sort of political bind?

- Are they resistant to making hard compromises?

- Do they have some feelings about you personally, technology in general, or your department that's standing in the way?

It is useful to jot these notes down or sketch them out in some way. Then think about the state you want them to be in to fulfill your goals. Imagine what needs to be different about them, about their knowledge, priorities, and attitudes. Identify the specific gaps that need to be addressed.

You will find some obstacles are opportunities in disguise. For example, if you are presenting to an egomaniac, you can work in acknowledgment of his team's achievements as an easy way to warm him up.

While it's important to consider the audience from all angles, as you go through your notes, some things will clearly be more important to address than others. Focus on those.

What do they really need to know?

Think about minimum information you need your audience to know to achieve your goal. This gives you a good sense of the maximum scope of the presentation. We geeks tend to cram everything we know into a presentation. It's a huge mistake.

We were recently at a conference where we attended what we thought would be a promising presentation, since we knew the presenter, and knew he was very smart. But for his 30-minute talk, he had prepared at least 60 slides, each with about 10 bullet points and a detailed (and too small to read) diagram. Of course, he only got through about five of those slides. Whatever his goal was, it wasn't accomplished. We left confused and disappointed, and he probably did too.

With information, there is a law of diminishing returns. People only retain a very small amount from a presentation, and the more information you put in, the less they retain. Think about the last two-day seminar you attended. What do you remember about what was said? I'll bet you can only come up with a few high-level bullet points and maybe a few details on one topic that really grabbed your attention.

You might not realize that for many business people, too many details get in the way of their understanding. They don't process information like geeks do. For geeks, details reveal truth, but for them, details cloud truth. They need an overview of things, something that they can relate to, rather than an onslaught of details that prove a point. Not only are too many details not helpful for them, but they interfere with their ability to grasp the big picture as well. Business people have patience for some level of detail, but only *after* they get the gist and can see the point.

It might help you to draft your presentation with all relevant details, since as a geek, you probably feel strongly that you need to back up what might feel to you like broad, sweeping statements. But bring forward the conclusions indicated by the details, and move the details to an appendix or a supporting document. We can assure you, those details might make you feel better, but your audience doesn't need them.

Believe it or not, business people are likely to trust your analysis, and extra details will probably diminish your credibility in their eyes.

What do they need to feel?

If you want your presentation to be transformational, you need to think about the emotional experience of the transition. You need to consider the feelings that will drive change forward and those that will block it. Getting a green light on a project calls for feelings of confidence, excitement, and hope. Putting a halt to an ill-conceived project calls for feelings of danger, dread, and a glimmer of hope for an alternative course. Getting people to use a newly rolled-out technology calls for feelings of hope, openness, and mastery.

Geeks don't like to think about making people feel things. They think feelings should be irrelevant at work. But they are not. In fact, for most people, especially business people, feelings are more potent than facts.

The writer Maya Angelou has observed that "people will forget what you said, people will forget what you did, but people will never forget how you made them feel." As keynote speakers, we've found this to be completely true. Paul has contacted people nearly a decade after a presentation. Despite the fact that they don't even recall the topic, they greet him warmly, remembering how much they enjoyed the experience.

So before you start to sequence your information, sequence the feelings that you want your audience to have. Start by predicting the feelings that they are bringing into the room, their initial state. Are they already angry, frustrated, excited, or indifferent? And where do you want them to go from there? Most importantly, where do you want them to end up?

Imagine that you are producing a silent movie. Envision the sequence of facial expressions that you want your audience to have as they change from the people they were before your session to the people they will become afterward. This sequence, this emotional arc, becomes the backbone of your presentation, the guide that drives its narrative structure.

Example of an emotional arc

We recently designed a new keynote presentation called "They Just Don't Get It: 7 Ways Geeks and Non-Geeks Can Get Along." We didn't start out by organizing the information. We started out by analyzing the experience we wanted the audience to have.

Here's the sequence we worked out. For each of the seven stages, we considered:

Thoughts – What are the audience members likely thinking about with respect to the topic and the presentation?

Questions – What questions or concerns are likely going through their heads?

Feelings – What are their dominant emotions?

Emotional Arc for Audience of "They Just Don't Get It"			
Stage	Thoughts	Questions	Feelings
1. Before it starts	Predicting possible outcomes	Will this be a good use of my time?	Slightly amused Dubious
2. Beginning	Assessing the problem and presenters	Is it relevant to me and my life?	Open Interested

3. Early middle	Gauging the importance of problem	Does this really matter?	Evaluative
4. Middle	Sensing the possibility of solution	Could that really help?	Engaged Surprised Reflective
5. Late middle	Weighing the practicality of suggestions	Could I really do that?	Intrigued
6. End	Committing to taking action in future	Why not give it a try?	Determined
7. After it ends	Reflecting on having spent time well, gotten value	Who else should hear this?	Satisfied Entertained Hopeful Enlivened Evangelical

CRAFT THE AUDIENCE TRANSFORMATION (WRITE IT)

The last part of preparing for the presentation is planning how you will facilitate the change in the audience and the situation. Some people call this writing the presentation, but if you think of it as a writing exercise, you'll probably go in the wrong direction. It's not about presenting information, but about facilitating change.

Your presentation has two key design criteria. Take this as seriously as if they were requirements for a technology product. The presentation must be designed to ensure that the audience will:

- Understand and retain the information
- Experience the sequence of emotions that lead to change

5 tips for making information easy to understand and remember

Here are a few of our general rules of thumb for presentation organization and preparation.

1. Discover how your audience likes to be communicated with

Every audience has different requirements for how they consume information. Presenting to marketers is different from presenting to finance people. They each have their own language and habits of thought that you need to respect. If you can, talk to someone who represents the audience beforehand and ask for some hints about how they consume information. Perhaps the best way to get at this information is to ask for examples of the most effective presentations they have experienced. Embedded in those stories are clues about what they need.

You might find that you are appalled at what they consider to be effective communication. But it won't help you to judge them. It will help you to put on your anthropologist hat and try to see it through their eyes. If the slide with three words and a smiley face really works for them, use it!

2. Don't write a reference guide

We've noticed that presentations are often organized around how the speaker thinks about the topic. For geeks, that usually means a well-ordered, highly structured, perfectly categorized list of all relevant information. This approach is great – if you're writing a reference book. Not so great if you want an audience to understand and retain what's important. It needs to be organized in a way that is easy to consume, not to refer to. There's a reason that people rarely read the Encyclopedia Britannica from front to back.

3. Use slides as headlines

PowerPoint is both a blessing and a curse for presenters. It can help the audience follow the flow of your presentation, but it can also draw their attention away from what you want to accomplish, and confuse them. The biggest mistake presenters make is using bullets as reminders of what they want to talk about. You end up using the slides as a script, and the audience gets distracted by reading and evaluating the information on the slide instead of listening to you. If the audience can get everything from the presentation by reading the slides, then you've put too much on them. The slides should just be there to serve as a visual cue as to what's important about what you're talking about. Think of slides as a series of headlines. We try to use less than 10 words on a slide.

4. Verbs are better than nouns

When you write your slides, you'll know that you're in the reference guide mode when you use nouns as headings. An overabundance of nouns as headings is not only boring, but also conveys a subtle pomposity, as if you are cataloging the way things are. Use verb phrases or questions as headings. They are more active. Verbs tell people what is happening or what they should do and why they should care.

5. Don't use slides as handouts

We have never had a good experience handing out copies of the slides at the start of the presentation. Sure, it seems like a good place for the audience to take personal notes, but what happens is that people read ahead. They don't realize it, but they are playing the "smartest-person-in-the-room game." They think, "Let me figure this out in the next five minutes and then spend the next 20 minutes thinking about questions that make me look good." Or they just look at their smartphone the rest of the time. If they pay attention to the handouts rather than to you, that's bad, because they are opting out of the emotional arc you created for them. So do them a favor and don't give them handouts. Keep them engaged with you, the topic, and your carefully crafted emotional arc. If they want the slides, hand them out at the end or email them later.

3 tools for eliciting emotions

As you organize your material, go back to the emotional arc you laid out for the audience and plan how you will create that experience. For each of the emotions, you will need to plan for how you are going to craft the opportunity for the audience to feel them.

Of course, you can't predict with perfect accuracy what any individual's emotional response will be to your presentation, but you can take a good guess. By analyzing the audience, you can plot out their likely reactions to what you have to say and structure the presentation to deliver the experience you want. To plan for creating that experience, think about the things that generate opportunities for emotional experiences for audiences. The three most common, in order of relative evocative power, are:

- Facts

- Insights

- Stories

1. Facts

Although facts are cold things, people who receive them are not. They may be surprised by them. They may deny the truth of the facts. They may become defensive. They may be awestruck, confused, angry, or smugly self-satisfied. Their reaction depends on the perspective they bring to the presentation.

For example, in our "They Just Don't Get It" presentation, we want the audience to feel the gravity of the disconnect between technical and non-technical people. So, early in the presentation, we show some statistics about project failure rates. As you can imagine, most people aren't shocked by the percentage of projects that fail. They have personal experience with that. They do seem more shocked by the fact that each year, U.S. businesses lose approximately $80 billion to failed IT projects.

But remember, facts are the weakest presentation tool for evoking emotions. Also notice that geeks tend to focus on facts and then wonder why no one seems affected by their presentations. Hmm.

2. Insights

The next most effective presentation tool is insight. These happen when the audience has an "aha moment." They experience this not because they learn some new individual fact, but because they either understand the significance of a fact – its implications – or because they connect multiple facts together in ways they hadn't before.

A common way of offering insight is to reason through something with the audience. You propose a set of facts and then walk them through an argument showing how they logically lead to a particular conclusion. Of course, geeks like this approach, because it's kind of like a mathematical proof.

To help the audience get the insight you are leading them to, you can use language cues. That way, they know to pay particular attention. You can say things like:

"You might be surprised to know that ..."

"Here's an often overlooked aspect ..."

"What really made my jaw drop was ..."

"Contrary to conventional wisdom ..."

"When you put all of this together ..."

The emotions people feel in response to insights are similar to their reactions to facts. You have to know what biases they bring to the presentation to predict what they will feel. But recognize that whatever emotions they experience, they probably won't be felt too deeply.

3. Stories

We're getting into considerably more powerful emotional territory with stories. Human beings are largely wired to think in narrative rather than in logic. Geeks often seem reluctant to use stories in their presentations, fearing that they may be perceived as time-wasting or manipulative.

Sometimes geeks avoid using stories because they think they are invalid as evidence. They cringe when they see people misuse anecdotes as if they were proof and harshly judge people for relying on them. They decide that they must be either idiots or manipulators. This unspoken judgment often gets in the way of their making use of this important rhetorical device.

Remember, the purpose of a story in a presentation is to illustrate points, synthesize ideas, and engage emotions. Anecdotes don't offer objective proof, but they invite the audience to have a subjective emotional experience that can be very persuasive.

3 important uses of story

1. Stories trigger a different way of knowing

Stories give the audience an opportunity to identify with the characters and situations you describe. People imagine themselves in the narrative, empathizing with the characters, feeling what they might feel. For many business people, this subjective experience is what they need in order to have the sense that they understand. For them, all the facts in the world are meaningless until there is some feeling associated with them.

This fundamental difference could largely account for the frustration geeks have when they communicate with business people. Most technical people have a decided preference for an objective way of knowing, one in which what is known is verifiable by something exterior to them. It may seem mysterious, and even wrong, that some people need to do a gut check before they can have the sense of "knowing." We suggest to you that, even though this is different from your preferred approach, it is not wrong, and it's important to make allowances for others' preferred style. If they need to relate the facts to something in their own experience, make it easy for them to do so. You're more likely to get the results you want.

2. Stories trigger memories

Audience members might recall a similar situation from their own past, briefly reliving whatever emotions were present for them in their own history. In recalling other memories and stories, they feel whatever they felt the first time they heard them. You can leverage that emotion to encourage the change you hoped to create.

For example, in some of our presentations, we reference John F. Kennedy's speech about sending a man to the moon. Most of the people in the room are too young to have experienced that triumph directly, but it lives on in movies and cultural memory as one of our country's proudest achievements. In hearing it referenced, we think of the tension and relief and awe-inspiring courage portrayed in the movies we have seen, such as *Apollo 13* or *The Right Stuff*. These associations, happening in rapid succession, create feelings of possibility that facts alone could never generate.

3. Stories show importance on a human scale

Sometimes big, scary numbers are motivating, but sometimes they can be overwhelming or make it seem as if it's someone else's problem. Think about how likely you are to help earthquake victims in Mexico versus the neighbor whose house just burnt down.

Here's another example. You might be motivated to take action by this statement: "Employees in our organization spend 2,000 hours a month filling out access request forms." But others might be more motivated by this one: "Last week, I spent three days trying to get my new employee access to the system. That's three days I wasn't doing my job and three days my employee was totally unproductive." The audience can readily put themselves in the shoes of the sufferer. Feeling her frustration, they feel a greater sense of urgency to fix the problem.

5 tips for using stories

Here are a few tips for good storytelling in presentation. Let's examine the same brief story told two different ways.

Tip	Instead of:	Try This:
Make it vivid. Use a *few* descriptive details to draw the audience into the world you create, to give the story a setting and make it emotionally engaging.	I was a project manager on a big financial system.	About 10 years ago, a large bank hired me to do project management during the development and testing phase of a loan management application.
Use dialog. Don't be afraid to act out a few lines. If the audience hears the characters' voices, they become more real.	Everyone blamed each other for the project failures.	Meanwhile, the developers would talk about the sponsors at lunch. "Serves them right for refusing to pay for a design cycle."

Get to the point. Too many details obscure your point and disengage the audience.	The project sponsors decided that they would only fund two weeks of planning before putting the coding out to bid for development vendors. The bids came in with a wide range of prices, and they chose the lowest bidder. So the development team started coding without thinking through the architecture.	I quickly realized that the project was doomed because they were coding without an architectural design.
Expose feelings. Don't just tell people what happened; tell them how the characters felt about what happened. A little information about feelings goes a long way toward drawing the audience into the characters' world.	During integration testing, they had to spend hundreds of thousands of dollars upgrading the server because nightly batch jobs took more than 24 hours to run.	Soon, the project sponsors were furious at the developers. Hundreds of thousands of dollars were being spent to upgrade the servers because nightly batch jobs took more than 24 hours to run.

Make it relevant. Too many speakers drop a story into a presentation because it's a great story, but if it's not really related to the points you're making, drop it. If it does relate, tell the audience exactly how. Don't assume that they'll get the point.	They ran way over budget, and the system never worked well.	So as you consider the time and cost for our design cycle, realize that it is a critical investment that really pays off.

PRESENT, CONNECT, RESONATE

Perhaps the most powerful tool for creating an emotional experience is personal resonance. That happens when the audience feels, at a visceral level, whatever it is that you are feeling. If you give your presentation with energy and enthusiasm, the audience will feel energized and enthusiastic. If you are distant and disinterested, they will be too.

Go back and watch an old video of Steve Jobs presenting a new product at an industry conference. He was a master of getting an audience to resonate with him. How does the audience seem to feel in response to his presentation? How do you feel while watching it? Think about how he created the excitement that was his trademark. Did he look disinterested and distant? Was he drily cataloging product specifications? Nope. He got the audience to share his feelings.

This is where you really put that emotional arc to work for you. At every point in your presentation, you know what you want the audience to feel. If you can feel it, they will feel it with you.

"Now, hold it just one minute," you might be saying. "I don't do feelings. That's why I write code!"

Don't worry. No one expects you to win an Academy Award for your presentation. You just need to be immersed in the emotional arc of your presentation, and to find ways – consistent with your personality – to bring this emotional arc to the foreground.

4 tips for connecting with your audience

1. Say it out loud

Give your audience verbal cues to what's happening emotionally

- "Here's the exciting part ..."
- "We've all been frustrated about this for some time ..."
- "I was astonished when I crunched the numbers ..."
- "I'm very proud of my team's work on this ..."

2. Let it show

There's an important distinction here. It's great to *let* emotion show. It could be deadly to *try* to show emotions. Deliberately acting out emotions holds the very real risk of appearing insincere. What you think is a smile could come off as a grimace, or when you think you're embodying frustration, you might inadvertently mystify people with an outburst of outrage.

3. Diffuse nervous energy

"But," you ask, "what if all I feel is nervous? Is that really what I want people to resonate with?" Actually, yes, briefly. Everyone has experienced being nervous in front of an audience, so they all know exactly what you're feeling. If you just acknowledge it, people will be sympathetic. And guess what – acknowledging it can make it go away. Now the audience is not to be feared, because you're all in the nervous boat together.

Paul does standup: The most nervous I ever got was performing a five-minute standup comedy routine at the Hollywood Improv. In the middle of my set, I completely forgot my jokes. After a long and uncomfortable pause, I pulled out my notes and made some comment about forgetting everything. Turns out it was the biggest laugh I got. They weren't laughing at me, but were genuinely sympathetic and enjoyed my honesty. (It's on YouTube, if you want to see my entire comedy career.)

4. Pause and look

The most powerful way to truly embody the emotional arc of the presentation is to pause and look. When you reach a particularly important point in your presentation, look at your audience to see if they are getting what you hoped. If they are, revel in it for a split second and experience the moment of silent agreement. The first few times you do this, you might find it shocking and a bit uncomfortable. Just stay with it; it gets better the more you get used to it.

You may make a bigger impact on your organization (and your career) in those half-seconds than you do with months of flawless coding or meticulous analysis. If your business audience resonates with you, that personal bond is invaluable in achieving your goals.

In short, the key points in evoking resonance are:

* Be yourself

- Be present

- Be aware of the importance of the substance of your presentation

- Pause to look at your audience

Conclude with a Call to Action

We've seen many well-organized and well-performed presentations fail to meet their goals because they flop at the end. They just peter out when the speaker runs out of time.

The message of your conclusion should not be, "I'm relieved to be done." You want to convey the idea that you are turning the responsibility for the transformation you want over to the audience. They need to know exactly what you want them to do next.

If you've designed the emotional arc correctly, the conclusion will be the moment when the audience feels most compelled to act. Don't let that moment go to waste. They will never be more committed to change than they are at the end of your presentation. If they don't know what to do with that determination, those feelings will dissipate and be forgotten before they get home for dinner.

Your last slide shouldn't be a generic one saying, "And now there's time for your questions." The last slide should have some specific call to action.

Think back to the common goals for presentations. Each one might have a different call to action. Here are a few examples in the following table.

Presentation goal	Possible call to action
Influence decisions	"I encourage you to select option A."
Manage expectations and share status	"Given that we are behind schedule, I would like you to write a prioritized list of the features from this phase, so that if we have to delay some, we'll know in advance which are likely to go."
Leverage opportunities	"Since it looks like we might be able to save a lot of money by moving our data center to the cloud, I think that we should assign Bob to evaluate the options and ask him to report back to us in two months with some estimates."
Leverage technology	"It's easy to forget what you've learned in this class today, so tomorrow, I'd like you to log into the test system and create three new contracts on your own."

The best-kept secret

And finally, we're going to tell you the best-kept secret about presenting to business people.

The audience is rooting for you. They want you to succeed. They want to feel good about the time they are investing with you. They want you to contribute to making their lives better. If you remember this and follow the guidelines in this article, you are sure to become a compelling and engaging presenter.

And who knows? The audience you dread the most might even become your biggest champions. (Business people are strange that way.)

OVERCOMING THE

INFLUENCE DEFICIT

This chapter delves into the question of why geeks lack influence and what they can do about it at a high level. The chapter that follows this one focuses on the personal skills you can develop to build influence in your organization.

One of the most poorly kept secrets of technology leadership is that geek leaders tend to lack influence in their organizations, especially in IT.

You've probably noticed that few IT leaders really seem to have the clout that you would think comes with their lofty titles, and a plausible explanation for this phenomenon is not apparent. But if you're interested in climbing the ladder, and being effective once you arrive at a higher rung, you need a useful framework for understanding why this might be happening and what you can do about it, so you can take your place in the inner circle of the organization.

In this chapter, we're going to look in depth at what influence is and why it is a particularly challenging part of a geek leader's job. In the next chapter, we'll explore the specific skills you need to become more influential. Both the explanation and the skills that we highlight are geared specifically toward people with technical backgrounds, because a lot of the generic approaches have not served us well.

Is it really that bad?

Unfortunately, it is. At all levels of IT management, leaders struggle to influence people in their organizations. You have probably experienced firsthand the frustration of not being able to get through to your colleagues, or wondered why your seat at the table seems to come with its own sound-canceling force field. It's puzzling. Business people hired you because you're the expert, and yet:

- They make decisions without consulting you.

- They often don't listen when they do consult you.

Geeks end up feeling confused, frustrated, and disrespected, wondering, "What's wrong with these people? Or worse, what's wrong with me?" The pain of disrespect is bad enough. When it's coupled with confusion about why it's happening and what to do about it, it is almost debilitating.

You are not alone in this experience. Every few years, there's a new study accompanied by a flurry of headlines reminding us about IT leaders' persistent lack of influence. Here are a few samples generated by a recent Gartner study:

- "CIOs dismissed as techies without business savvy by CEOs" *Computerworld UK*, April 12, 2012

- "Why CIOs Are Last Among Equals"
  Sloan Management Review, May 20, 2012

- "Most CIOs on the board but have little business
  influence" *Computerworld UK*, July 20, 2012

What's been tried to fix this?

Geek leaders are not ones to leave a problem unsolved. And they have been diligently working on this problem for a generation. They have invested countless hours learning to "speak the language of the business," with the assumption that if they do that, they will be heard and their influence will be embraced. They've gotten MBAs and other advanced degrees hoping that the credentials will bolster their stature as authorities, which, in turn, will make people listen more. They have devised ingenious metrics to measure and prove their worth, with the assumption that when people understand how important we are to the mission of the organization, they will listen.

But year after year, very little changes.

WHY GEEKS LACK INFLUENCE

Perhaps nothing changes because geeks haven't grasped the underlying reasons for why they have lacked influence for so long. These reasons have been hiding in places where geeks tend not to look: in the realms of human relationships, trust, and empathy. In our work exploring the worldview differences between geeks and non-geeks, we have uncovered unexpected insights about why IT professionals tend to lack influence.

The primary reasons include:

- Geeks don't know the difference between influence and power.

- Geeks fail to cultivate the preconditions for being influential.

- Geeks try to use techniques that are more suited to salespeople than geeks.

Influence vs. power

The biggest reason that geeks don't have much influence is that they fundamentally misunderstand what it is. They have trouble, as most people do, distinguishing between influence and power.

When we lead discussions with senior IT leaders – even groups of CIOs – and ask them to describe the difference between influence and power, they quickly become flustered and confused by their lack of clarity. They usually assert that both are a means of getting people to do what you want. And in this model, influence becomes a kind of watered-down version of power, a kind of power-lite. With power, you just tell people what to do and they do it because you control the consequences of their compliance. With influence, you ask, cajole, or persuade them to do it instead.

But that model is incorrect. Power and influence are not different means for achieving the same end. They are quite distinct from one another, and if you want to expand your ability to influence people, you need to understand the difference.

Power is the ability to affect another person's *observable behavior.*

If I'm wielding power, I have the means and will to coerce you to do what I want. I may do it through authority, control of rewards, or threats of punishment, but regardless, it is coercive.

Influence is the ability to affect another person's *inner state* – what they think, feel, and believe.

If I'm exerting influence, I'm trying to change your inner experience, how you think or feel about something. Perhaps you may do something differently because of your internal change, but it's not because I "made you do it."

Let's look at an everyday example of the difference between power and influence. You pick up your mail and see that you have been summoned to jury duty. You know that if you don't show up you could be fined or even jailed. And you know that the state, with its well-funded police force, could nab you the next time you run a stop sign, and the consequences could be severe. So despite the huge inconvenience, you show up at jury duty, grumbling all the way. The police and judge really couldn't care less what your inner state might be, whether you're happy to serve or not. All they care about is your compliance.

Let's say you are picked to sit on that jury. Now you are listening to the lawyers present their case, trying to sway your opinion toward their side in whatever way they can. But these lawyers have no power over you. All they can do is influence how you view the facts, how you feel about the defendants, and what principles of right and wrong you should apply.

As you can see, the targets are completely different. With power, your inner state is irrelevant. With influence, your inner state is everything.

The preconditions of influence

Given that influence is about affecting someone's inner state, we can now see how the requirements for exercising influence are very different than simply having a carrot or a stick. There are three basic preconditions that must be met by you and the people you want to influence.

- They must be *open* to being influenced by you.

- You must be *willing* to change their inner state.

- You must be *able* to move them to think, feel, and/or believe differently.

The hard truth is that many technical leaders lack influence because they don't meet the preconditions of influence. They rarely consider whether or not people are open to them. And since they have an aversion to meddling in people's inner lives, they are neither willing nor particularly capable of doing it well.

Why? Because they prefer to believe that facts should be influential, not people.

Facts aren't enough

Early in Paul's consulting career, he had a painful lesson in which facts, logic, and reason completely failed him. Here's his story:

A CIO hired me to fix his department's software development process problems. Specifically, he wanted me to analyze why, despite having implemented elaborate processes, the projects were still late, over budget, or failing altogether.

So I did my analysis and felt good about my conclusions. I wrote a detailed and logically organized presentation, and walked the CIO through it. As I presented it, he seemed engaged, receptive, and pleased. He asked good questions and constantly nodded in agreement with key points. In short, he agreed with the facts. He agreed with principles. He agreed with absolutely everything I said – until I got to the recommendations.

When I started to recommend specific changes, including some behavioral adjustments for him, his demeanor completely changed. With a scowl on his face he said, "I'm not doing any of that."

I was totally shocked. Hadn't I laid out a rational, reasonable case supported by credible evidence, and hadn't he agreed with every premise and every fact? Yes on both counts. So what went wrong?

In retrospect, I realized I hadn't prepared him emotionally to accept that what he thought were process problems were really people problems, in which he played an important role. I made the mistake of assuming that the indisputable facts would lead to the obvious conclusion and compel him to take action. But I failed to move him in the direction of making a personal change, and nothing got better.

This is not a unique experience. When we tell this story at workshops and presentations, heads nod in recognition. It is an almost universal experience among geek leaders: Though we may have masterful command over the facts, we often fail to influence the people, even when it is for their own good.

Ill-fitting advice

While geeks overemphasize the importance of facts and overlook the importance of cultivating emotional openness, experts on influence tend to overemphasize the importance of persuasive techniques and overlook the importance of overcoming resistance to even using these techniques.

Many useful and widely read books have been written on influence and persuasion, and what they tend to have in common is that they focus on skills and techniques. We've observed that blindly following this type of advice rarely leads to influence, at least for technical people. Those who try to use these formulaic approaches seem wooden and inauthentic, odd and off-putting.

Many of the techniques are about overwhelming other people's resistance to your will, or treating others like unwitting victims of your savvy manipulation. While this may be fine for a salesperson trying to close a single deal, it's not the kind of approach most geeks can adopt.

Geeks are generally not interested in dominating others. They want to be respected and included, not feared and obeyed. Nor are they interested in manipulating how people feel. Many geek leaders very strongly adhere to principles of respect for others' intelligence, transparency of information and intent, and rational decision-making based on good facts. So telling them to simply adopt persuasive techniques without addressing their aversion to persuading other people won't help much.

HOW GEEKS CAN BECOME MORE INFLUENTIAL

So what geek leaders need is an approach that:

- Is focused on building influence rather than power
- Is consistent with their goals and personalities
- Works both for them and for those they would like to influence

What we've observed is that rather than following the conventional advice, a more effective approach is to think about influence as a two-stage process for meeting the preconditions for influence:

- First reduce resistance
- Then use techniques of influence to change others' inner state

Now, let's look at the preconditions for influence and note that this approach addressees all three and raises the probability of success.

REDUCE *YOUR* RESISTANCE: BECOME WILLING TO MOVE PEOPLE

The first source of resistance isn't theirs, but yours. Geeks hate the whole idea of influence, once they understand what it really means. You might be saying to yourself, "Don't be absurd; of course I'm willing to influence people. I wouldn't be reading about it if I weren't."

But don't be so sure.

Your beliefs undermine your willingness

If you are like many people in technology, you probably hold some firm beliefs that get in the way of your willingness to move people. We've identified two beliefs that are real obstacles.

1. People's decisions should be based on logic and objectively verifiable facts rather than subjective experience.

Most geeks believe that how people feel on the inside, their subjective reality, is not a good basis for decision-making. It's irrelevant at best and destructive at worst. Geeks love working with technology because, unlike people, it behaves predictably and consistently (usually). In their heart of hearts, they dearly wish that people would behave this way, too. What they really wish is that influence was unnecessary and that we would all look at the same set of facts and independently come to the same conclusion. That human beings don't behave this way seems to them like a design flaw.

So geeks carry around the sense that humans who don't operate on pure reason are flawed (and annoying).

2. "Manipulating" other people's inner experience is wrong.

Geeks don't want to take advantage of a design flaw. They don't want to appeal to how people feel on the inside, because it seems disrespectful, like pointing out that someone has something stuck in his teeth. They have a negative emotional reaction to the whole idea of appealing to emotions, since they hate it when people appeal to theirs.

It is a weird irony that geeks' reputation for being mechanical and robotic is based on their most empathetic impulse. They don't appeal to emotions because it makes them cringe to have their emotions appealed to, and they really don't want to do that to other people.

These beliefs, which may be very important to developing great technology, undermine geeks' influence, because, as we will see, many if not most of their colleagues rely on their emotions to understand the world and make decisions.

Geeks' unwillingness to try to change others' emotions is at the heart of why they lack influence.

Decisions are based on emotions

As much as geeks wish it weren't so, human emotions are essential to decision-making. Reason, facts, and logic just aren't enough. At a very basic level, human organisms determine what to do next by distinguishing what feels good from what feels bad. And the experience of good and bad, rewarding and punishing, is a function of how we process simple emotional responses. When emotional processing is damaged, people become paralyzed with indecision.

Some of the most compelling evidence of this comes from the work of a neuroscientist named Antonio Damasio. He studied a number of patients with damage to part of the orbitofrontal cortex and a portion of the prefrontal cortex, the part of the brain associated with emotional processing.

He noticed that these patients not only became emotionless and devoid of wants and desires, but also became utterly unable to make decisions. One day, one of his emotionless patients, whom the psychology world knows as Eliot, tried to make a simple decision about when to set up his next appointment with the researcher. This is how Damasio describes it:

"For the better part of half an hour, the patient enumerated reasons for and against each of the two dates: previous engagements, proximity to other engagements, possible meteorological conditions, virtually anything that one could reasonably think about concerning a simple date. [It was] a fruitless comparison of options and possible consequences. It took enormous discipline to listen to all of this without pounding on the table and telling him to stop."

Numerous other studies are shedding light on how simple affective experience enables cognition. But let's look at a very simple model for how this works, because accepting the role of emotions in decision-making is essential for becoming more willing to move people toward good decisions.

A geek-compatible approach to appealing to emotions

Emotions are hard to understand and deal with. They seem infinitely complex, completely unpredictable, and inherently ambiguous. But there is one rule of thumb that we have found to be extremely useful for concrete thinkers who want to up their emotional game. Simply put:

> People choose things that make them feel good or
> not feel bad.

With this rule of thumb, you can adjust your approach to influencing someone based on what makes him feel good. And the first step toward doing so is to recognize this important truth:

What makes you feel good does not necessarily make someone else feel good.

This seems like it's almost too obvious to bother saying, but you would be surprised how often we lose sight of this basic fact, especially at work. And in our exploration of the differences between geeks and non-geeks, we've identified a fundamental difference in what geeks find rewarding compared to most of the rest of the work world.

This difference is marked by how deeply rewarding it is for geeks to align themselves with Truth. Objectively verifiable truth. For many geeks, this is their primary means of connecting with other people. By sharing agreement on what is known to be true, they feel a sense of belonging to a community greater than themselves.

So geeks, ironically, have a very emotional attachment to facts and logic, because that feels good. It's no accident that Mr. Spock is by far the most popular *Star Trek* character of all time among geeks.

Other people are not necessarily motivated by objectivity in the same way. Let's look at some differences:

Objectivity makes geeks feel good	Non-geeks gravitate toward the subjective and social
Facts	Belonging
Logic	Status
Evidence	Harmony
Analysis	Self-expression
Right answers	Winning

While it is not in our scope to describe the entirety of possible human motivations, we highlight some that you will likely see at work – motivations that value social standing and subjective experience much more than geeks do. And as commonplace as these social and subjective motivations are, we find that many geeks refuse to accept their validity as motives.

To geeks, the desire for self-expression seems indulgent. Status-seeking seems craven, belonging seems trivial, harmony seems pathetically Pollyannaish, and winning seems evil.

Since these alternative motivations seem so wrong, then appealing to them feels even more wrong. Many geek leaders are unwilling to do so, and this is at the heart of why they lack influence – because they aren't willing to extend themselves, stretch their worldviews, and meet people where they are.

One could look at this tendency negatively and label it stubbornness and inflexibility, but we prefer to recognize that this tendency is rooted in strong principled behavior and a special geek brand of empathy. Geeks are simply following the Golden Rule here: treating others as they would like to be treated.

But the Golden Rule is fundamentally flawed, because it doesn't account for real, deep, divisive differences in what people find rewarding.

REDUCE THEIR RESISTANCE: FOSTER OPENNESS

The second source of resistance is theirs rather than ours. No matter how willing you are to change other people's inner experience, they must be willing to allow us to do that. You can't overpower someone to change how he feels. You can't grab your project sponsor by the shirt, stare into his eyes, and say, "You will care about this project now."

So we need to understand what makes a person open to being influenced by someone else. It's rather simple, really. To be open to your influence, a person needs to *believe* two things:

- You are competent enough to help me in this domain.

- You are on my side.

Just as geeks overemphasize facts, they also tend to overemphasize competence. They believe that if they are knowledgeable in this area and smart, then people should be open to their influence. In other words, "If I know what I'm talking about, you should listen."

That's why geeks spend so much time and effort demonstrating, validating, and expanding their competence. They love achieving advanced degrees, learning new skills, and getting certified in a new languages or project management approaches. For geeks, these things are fun and satisfying in themselves, but geeks also believe that they are the things that should matter most to others whom they want to be open to their influence. The idea they cannot shake is this: "If an objective third party deems me competent, then so should you."

But this single-minded focus on competence has disastrous results. Because, in truth, if the person you want to influence doesn't think you're on his side, then it doesn't matter what he thinks of your competence. In fact, if he thinks that your allegiance lies elsewhere and also considers you competent, he becomes even less open. Competent enemies are much more threatening than incompetent ones.

So we're not going to focus on competence here, since that's not our challenge. Let's focus on the second criterion, because, in general, we are terrible at creating the feeling in others that we are "on their side."

"That's absurd," you say. "How could they doubt my commitment? Don't they know how many hours I put in? While they're home watching a football game, my team and I are here launching services for them."

Well, actually, they don't know the number of hours that you put in, and even if they did, that's not how people evaluate whether or not you are on their side.

How do people evaluate same-sidedness?

The source of the feeling of same-sidedness is primal, even bio-logical, and is sensed by people based on a number of cues that we geeks rarely attend to.

This is because the *feeling* of "being on your side" is rooted in our nature as social animals. We evolved as tribal creatures, and determining who was in and out of our circle of support was critical to survival. As animals we needed to know:

* Who would help us survive and deserves to be helped by us

* Who would harm us and deserves to be killed, enslaved, or avoided

It's an instinctive feeling, not a rational calculation. And it's a feeling that's primarily triggered by empathy.

Empathy is the key to openness

Our human physiology bears evidence of the importance of de-termining who is on our side and who is not.

In the late 1990s, brain scientists discovered that a consider-able portion of the human brain was composed of what they now call "mirror neurons," whose function is to recognize and reproduce the emotional experience of other people. Before that, it was assumed that the brain had three major functions: memory, cognition, and autonomic control.

But it became clear that there was more. It now seems that another major function is creating the ability to put yourself in someone else's shoes. When we see other people do things like reach for a peanut or get poked with a stick, the corresponding neurons in our own brains become activated, as if we ourselves were experiencing that sensation, or executing that action.

"Any time you watch someone doing something, the neurons that your brain would use to do the same thing become active – as if you yourself were doing it," explains neuroscientist V.S. Ramachandran.

This capacity benefits us in many ways, allowing us to

Imitate others seamlessly, enabling easy transmission of knowledge and culture. If he hits a rock like that against another rock, and a spark jumps out, then I can do that very same thing. In fact, I'm already doing it in my mind, so I think I'll make myself some fire.

Predict intentions of other people; recognize and advance their goals: If I were looking longingly at those grapes hanging from a vine just beyond my reach, you would know instinctively I want those grapes. And knowing that, you instinctively realize that if you give me a boost, I'll reach them, and be gratified and grateful to you.

Learn language: If mom puts her lips that way, and I put my lips that way, I'm going to make a sound like she makes, and – look! – I'm doing it and it makes her happy!

And our mirror neurons don't fire equally for just anyone. Research is beginning to indicate that the closer the affiliation between people, the more strongly their mirror neurons fire. So the closer you feel to someone, the more intensely you feel his pain and want to avoid causing it. And the more we detect that someone else resonates with our emotions, the more we trust that they are on our side.

In short, we look for cues of empathetic feelings as a sign that it is safe to be open to someone's influence.

Empathy is constantly being reassessed

"Oh, no," you might be thinking. "If I wanted a job where empathy mattered, I would have become a social worker or a salesman. Now you tell me that to create good technology I have to show people that I care about them?"

Actually, yes. Sorry.

But wait. It gets worse. Not only is empathy required, but it's not a one-time thing.

Same-sidedness is something that we constantly monitor and reassess. You may feel that I'm on your side today and feel completely differently tomorrow based on your subconscious assessment of my empathy.

This collides with another geek cultural bias. Geeks tend to see the world through the lens of problems and solutions. And once a problem is solved, it stays solved. The idea that the right answer to a question can change from day to day is profoundly disturbing. A geek would assume that once someone believes that he is on her side, the question is settled and they can move on to other things.

But if you want to be influential, you need to recognize that this is not a problem that can be solved, but a situation to be managed. The question of whether others feel as if we are on their side will never go away.

Non-verbal cues that I am on your side:	Verbal cues that I am on your side:
Looking	I understand
Nodding	You seem worried about that
Smiling	I want to know more
Head tilting	That must be difficult
Not interrupting	I want to help
Leaning in	I'm interested in that too

How we inadvertently close them off

When a geek encounters others' resistance to his influence, he has a quite natural emotional response to their resistance. He knows that he is on their side. There's little that is more maddening than being treated as if you are an enemy when you know that you are a friend. It feels irrational.

In addition, when geeks' influence is spurned, they assume that their competence is being called into question, since geeks believe that competence should lead to influence. And since geeks value competence so highly, they get insulted.

And a common response to being insulted by another person is to feel contempt for that person.

"Well, maybe so," you say. "But I am very careful to treat everyone I work with respectfully. I would never treat anyone with contempt."

And for that we applaud you. A commitment to respect is a powerful character strength and essential to fostering influence.

But you should know that contemptuous thoughts can rarely be hidden.

For as much as people need to be hit across the side of the head with evidence that you share their concerns, they are incredibly sensitive to any sign that someone views them negatively. And contempt is very difficult to conceal; sometimes, the very attempt to conceal it – flat voice and stony face – is exactly what betrays its presence. People's mirror neurons pick up your contempt whether you like it or not.

And when they sense contempt rather than empathy, they become convinced that you're not on their side and resist you even more.

To reduce contempt, you need to catch it in the act. The clue that you're falling into this trap is when you hear yourself thinking about another person and the word "should" comes to mind. "They *should* do this." Or, "they *shouldn't* believe something like that." When you notice that, you're in danger of slipping into contempt. It indicates that you feel that there's a right and wrong way to approach something and you're going to judge the idiots who do it wrong. You need to accept that they are different from you and see the world differently.

Empathy paves the way

Much later in Paul's career, having learned the limitations of the fact-only approach to influence, he had an opportunity to use empathy as an explicit strategy to build influence with a client. It resulted in saving the client millions of dollars. Here's the story:

A CIO of a midsized manufacturing firm hired me to figure out what to do with a botched ERP implementation. Among the many detractors of this system, the most vociferous were the manufacturing operations people, whose angry cries to have it replaced immediately were deafening, even though they were 1,000 miles from headquarters.

After a couple of weeks of analysis, it became clear that replacing the system didn't make sense. It would cost more than $3 million and offer no business value over fixing the one already in place. But how could I build consensus around this decision when so many of the stakeholders were collecting pitchforks for a march on the corporate office?

In my younger days, I would have put together a cogent, logically structured, well-organized presentation to convince them to support my recommendations. But this time I knew better. Instead, I planned a four-day trip to the manufacturing facility, the only goal being to meet their preconditions for influence, to reduce their resistance to me and my recommendations.

I needed them to know that I was on their side, that I understood their needs and cared about them as people and colleagues. And since I was presumed to be tainted by my association with the hated system, I also needed them to accept that I was competent to help. So I made sure we had enough face time, scheduling two hours with each of the key managers. In meetings, I emphasized that I had no personal agenda, explaining that I had no opinion about the right course of action until I had consulted with them. I created an opportunity for empathetic listening by asking a single open-ended question about their experience of the implementation and working with the product.

At each stakeholder meeting, a tidal wave of anger and complaints crashed down on me.

I didn't attempt to refute anything they said. I only listened patiently, took notes, and asked clarifying questions. I let myself be moved by the magnitude of what they had suffered, and sincerely offered sympathetic statements like, "That sounds awful," or, "I can see why you'd be so angry about that."

At the end of each meeting, I explained that I would go back and complete my analysis and return in a few weeks with a proposed course of action. And I assured them that whatever I recommended, I was committed to making sure their needs were met this time.

This trip was not about gathering information. I got a pretty good picture of the facts of the situation in the first half-day, and then spent three and a half days listening to the same stories over and over.

But by the end of the four days, a remarkable transformation had happened. The manufacturing team still despised the system, but they were no longer intensely resistant to me, my boss, and anything we had to say. I hadn't fully convinced them that I was on their side, but I had shifted their stance from outright hostility to guarded optimism.

Two weeks later, when I returned and gave them the logical structured presentation that I could have given on the first visit, they accepted that it was the best course of action, and they agreed to support it. They weren't overjoyed about the conclusion, but were open to accepting it because they trusted that my analysis was done with their needs and objectives in mind.

Without that first trip to meet their preconditions for openness, I have no doubt that they would not have accepted the recommendations and likely would've thrown me out of the building. Those few days of listening, where very little was done and very little was learned, resulted in the company saving millions of dollars.

WHAT PAUL DID TO SAVE MILLIONS OF DOLLARS

So what were the cues of same-sidedness that I offered in those meetings at the manufacturing site?

I took lots of notes so they could see me writing down what they said.

I looked directly at them without avoidance or shame.

I nodded my understanding.

I mirrored their body language, leaning in when they did, leaning back when they didn't.

I didn't interrupt or defend.

I asked clarifying questions.

I commented on their emotions: "That must've been really frustrating."

In this case, a little bit of empathy went a long way toward fostering their openness to influence.

NOW YOU'RE READY
TO START INFLUENCING

So now, after all this reducing resistance to influence on both sides of the relationship, you're finally ready to do what you set out to do: become more influential. In the next chapter, we'll cover some basic approaches and techniques that are both effective and compatible with our geek personalities.

5 SOFT SKILLS FOR

INFLUENCING

BUSINESS PEOPLE

If you skipped directly to this chapter looking only for "what to do" to become more influential, we encourage you to read the previous chapter first. We admire your action- and goal-oriented approach, but techniques are just tools. To use them effectively, you need a firm understanding of why you would use these and not others, why you haven't used them before, and when each is appropriate. For many people, influence skills come naturally. But for geeks, not so often. Until you grapple with the beliefs that limit your ability to be influential, even the best techniques in the world will not work for you. So go read the previous chapter. We'll wait….

Welcome back! Aren't you glad you went back and read that chapter?

In the last chapter, we saw that IT leaders lack influence in their organizations because they often misunderstand what influence is and don't meet the preconditions for it.

- We must be willing to move people to change what they think, feel, or believe.

- We must foster their willingness to be open and trusting of our input and suggestions.

Now we are ready to look at the five essential soft skills that you need to become more influential.

WHAT ARE SOFT SKILLS, ANYWAY?

Influence skills fall into that dreaded category: soft skills. We have all heard, at one point or another, that to advance our careers we need to improve our soft skills.

So we dutifully sign up for the soft-skills seminars, holding our noses and rolling our eyes, wishing that we could focus on "real" work. And it's not surprising, given that this territory is plagued by loose definitions and confusion. If you try to clarify what soft skills are by looking at the endless websites devoted to exploring them (or selling training programs), you'll get confused rather quickly. Here are a few representative examples:

- "Soft skills mean manners and how you hold yourself in public."

- "They are the character traits and interpersonal skills that characterize a person's relationships with other people."

- "Soft skills are basically social skills, sometimes known as people skills or interpersonal skills."

While all of these definitions touch on elements of soft skills, they fail to meet the standards of clarity that geeks expect and demand. And more importantly here, these vague definitions are not particularly useful when you're trying to figure out what you need to do to be more influential.

Since it seems so difficult to define soft skills directly, let's start with its opposite, hard skills.

Hard skills are the technical skills you need to get your job done.

Whatever it is you produce, hard skills are the ones that you need to produce it. You may need to know SQL or C++. You may need to have knowledge of software development processes and project management tools. You may need a mastery of writing user manuals in language accessible to the user base.

Soft skills, on the other hand, are what you need to use your hard skills effectively. You won't write good code if you can't get an understanding of what it's for. You won't get sponsors to set priorities if you can't help them understand their options. You won't get any referrals for new work if you can't manage stakeholder expectations about launch dates and feature sets.

In short, hard skills are for producing work, and soft skills are for affecting other people's experience of working with you, so that you can produce work.

As such, we would like to propose a clearer definition of soft skills, one that emphasizes the real purpose for employing them.

Soft skills are what you use to influence other people's experience.

The reason that we like this definition is that it captures what's really important about soft skills, which is that they are about changing other people's inner experience in ways that support getting your job done.

SO WHICH SOFT SKILLS ARE ESSENTIAL FOR INFLUENCE?

To understand which soft skills are essential for influence, we need to think carefully about what technical leaders actually produce.

The primary role of technical leaders is not to produce concrete technical deliverables. They may write reports, presentations, and plans, but those do not fulfill the goals of the role. Technical leaders are successful when their projects are successful; when the technology is produced on time, on budget, and to scope; and when it produces tangible benefits for the users. So it seems rather natural to conclude that technical leaders lead technology. But this conclusion wreaks havoc with how geek leaders understand their jobs.

Technology, an inanimate object, cannot be led. It can be imagined, created, and debugged – by people.

Only people can be led. Therefore, we need to understand our jobs in terms of the people we lead, not the technology we create. Simply stated:

The primary job of a technical leader is to *create the conditions* under which *people* can produce and support *great technology*.

While the conditions under which people can be productive might include providing the physical resources required, such as desks, computers, meeting rooms, and technical tools, the most difficult and subtle aspect of the job is to create the emotional conditions under which people can be creative and productive.

So creating the conditions for productivity is primarily about influencing other people's inner state, helping them to focus on the task at hand and access their creativity and drive. Therefore:

For technical leaders, soft skills are the hard skills.

And perhaps hardest of all are influence skills. It's when you serve as your group's representative to the outside world – to stakeholders, managers, executives, users, and vendors – that you need to influence people most: to get resources, to build consensus on goals, and to gain support for compromises between schedule, budget, and features. This is when you need the influence skills to get these things from people who do not think like geeks and don't necessarily believe that you are on their side.

And that leads us to the soft skills that are important for influence, skills that will create for other people the experience of being open to you and trusting of your input.

Here are the five soft skills we have found to be most important for tech leaders to work on for expanding their influence:

1. Listen for what is important to people
2. Describe a rosy future
3. Expose your desire
4. Express commitment
5. Translate facts into stories

We will explore each one in more detail and explain both why it is important and what you need to do to enhance your abilities.

SKILL #1: LISTEN FOR WHAT'S IMPORTANT TO PEOPLE

This is the single most important technique for reducing resistance to your influence. If you're only going to focus your energy on developing one skill for influence, this is it. So we're going to invest more time with this one than with the others.

What "listening for what's important" is, and why it matters

When you listen for what's important to another person, you are trying to understand not just what they tell you literally, but what really matters to them about the current situation.

This is an important tool of influence because:

To change someone's inner experience meaningfully, you need to understand his current state. You need to know what about his experience you want to change.

The experience of being deeply listened to – of being understood – is a powerful cue that both parties are on the same side. People's responses to feeling understood or misunderstood are intense and visceral. Even if they can't state clearly what's important to them, they surely know when someone else neither understands nor shares their sense of what's important. The feeling that comes with not being understood can be intense and painful. And similarly, the feeling that comes with being understood can be highly pleasurable.

Think about how this feels to you.

* Think about a time when someone really "got" something important you were trying to tell her. You

were struggling for words to say something complex, and your listener paraphrased it in exactly the right way. How did you feel when you realized that she understood? Relieved? Satisfied? Safe? Encouraged?

- Now think back to when someone simply wouldn't or couldn't understand something important to you. You tried again and again to get her to see why it was worth caring about, but her puzzled expression made it clear she just never would. How did you feel at that moment? Frustrated? Impatient? Isolated? On guard?

- Now consider which of these people you would rather be influenced by: the one who understands what's important to you or the one who is either unable or unwilling?

Your job is to detect what problems people care most about solving. Doing so moves them both rationally and emotionally. Here's what it's like for them.

If I know that you know what is important to me ...	
Reason	I can more confidently predict that I'll get what I want, even if I have difficulty articulating it.
Emotion	I'll trust that you are supporting me personally – that you are on my side, not just buying in to my objectives.

In short, people trust you if they feel that you understand what is important to them, even if you don't entirely agree with them. They don't trust you if they feel that you don't understand. And they feel contempt for you if they think you don't care enough to try to understand.

Not quite the same as active listening

Chances are that you've heard of a technique called active listening. It involves patiently hearing out what someone is saying and paraphrasing what you heard back to him. It's a very useful technique, because not only do you confirm the information, but the person you're talking to registers that you understood as well.

Listening for what's important to other people is similar, but extends the approach even further. Here, you are not only listening for what they say, but more importantly listening for what they mean.

You're listening for:

* What they say

* What they don't say

* What they don't know how to say

People don't often come right out and declare what they care about. It is your responsibility to tease it out and reflect back to them what you understood to be important to them. Once you understand, you can validate its importance to you.

Why we resist

Geeks often deliberately reject this type of listening, especially when it comes to getting requirements from non-technical stakeholders. It's because they hold certain beliefs, derived from the development and support processes that they've been taught. We believe:

- They *should* know what they want.

- They *should* articulate what's important to them.

- They *should* translate what's important to them into technology requests.

- What they tell us *should* be precisely and literally true.

Notice all the "shoulds" in these beliefs. Geeks serve the needs of their stakeholders, who should be the source of requirements and requests. Unfortunately, real people don't always work that way.

To master the skill of listening for what is important, you must allow that people frequently fall short of these ideals. They often:

- Don't know exactly what they want. For many people, this becomes clear to them in the course of a conversation.

- Avoid actually stating what they really care about, and instead make specific requests that they presume will best address the issue. In short, they ask for a solution to an unarticulated problem.

- Lack sufficient knowledge about technology to make informed requests without help.

- Speak imprecisely. They don't express themselves fully. People frequently use metaphors, guesses, and half-truths.

How to find what's important to people

You might be wondering, "If people won't or can't say what they care about, how the heck am I supposed to know?" The secret is to look for signs of emotion. Here's a simple rule:

Where there is emotion, there is importance.

People don't have feelings about unimportant things, so if you follow the feelings, you'll find what they care about. Once you notice the emotions in their statements, intonation, or language, you can use all of your powers of deductive and inductive reasoning to make your best guess about what underlies their feelings.

Here are four essential elements for this skill.

Observe

Signs of emotion are easy to spot if you remind yourself that you should be looking for them. The basic expressions of human emotion are instinctive and common, so it's just a matter of paying attention to something we typically consider unimportant or even inappropriate at work. So when you are listening, look for signs of:

Positive affect

- *Excitement and enthusiasm* – High energy, big smile, emphatic gestures

- *Interest* – Sly grin, questions, returning to same point

Negative affect

- *Anger* – Pursed lips, furrowed brow

- *Frustration* – Sigh, clenched teeth

- *Stubbornness* – Not listening

- *Irrationality* – (Your confusion)

The key is knowing that the emotions may not be directly related to what the person is saying at the time he displays it. An especially good cue is when the intensity of emotion he displays does not fit with the content of what he's saying. If someone is red in the face, screaming, and upset about some minor issue, chances are that what he's complaining about isn't really what's bothering him. You'll need to dig deeper to find out what it really is.

Once you see the emotions, you have several options for how to figure out what important things are eliciting these emotions.

Ask

There is absolutely no harm in asking someone what she cares about. These types of questions are usually welcomed. People are often glad to be asked to talk about what is important to them.

Try asking some very simple questions like the following:

- "What is most important *to you* about this project?"
- "What will make you feel like this has really worked?"
- "What worries you about the plans?"

Notice that this is very different from asking about goals or objective project success criteria. Geeks often ask people to rank their priorities (features, budget, schedule, quality). But the brain circuits that give you access to what you care about are not the same brain circuits that allow you to rank things in relative order. It's like the difference between

"How's your son's robot project coming along?"

and

"How many hours have you spent on your son's robot project?"

One is open-ended and invites excitement and pride. Open-ended questions make room for people to talk about their subjective experience. The other taps into the calculating parts of the brain and is not likely to engender an emotional response. Both types of questions have their place, but when asking about importance, you want to stay in the realm of emotions.

Postpone objections

While you are listening to someone talk about what he wants or what he is interested in, you might be tempted to voice your concerns about the plausibility and risks. You might even be tempted to test the validity of the request by exploring exceptions and edge cases, right then and there. As problem-solvers, we do this all the time. But this form of analysis is destructive to influence when done at the wrong time. There are two reasons for this:

People hear our problem-solving as resistance and negativity. Rather than experiencing our questions and analysis as a form of support, they hear it as judgment of their competence.

It interrupts their flow of thought, which feels bad and disrespectful. When they are struggling to articulate what's important to them, interruptions can be disruptive and even painful. It's a similar experience to the one we have when we get interrupted in the middle of writing code. How long does it take you to get back to where you were and become productive again? That's what it's like for someone who is trying to explain his vision for a product or imagine the features he needs when you interrupt.

Before you start to question a request, make sure you've confirmed that you understand what's important about it. Once the business person knows that you're looking to understand before evaluating, she can participate in the evaluation with you rather than feeling judged and belittled. A surefire approach to postponing objections is to always have paper and pen handy. You can jot your thoughts down and come back to them after you have made sure that the other person has been heard.

Reflect & confirm

In active listening, you reflect back the literal meaning of what you heard. In listening for what's important, you'll be reflecting a reasoned guess as to what is important about what the other person was saying. You will be making assumptions about someone else's inner life. You will be forming hypotheses about what's important to her and respectfully asking if you're correct.

And you'll probably open your response with a simple phrase like:

- It sounds like what you want is …

- It seems to be really important to you that …

- If I understand correctly, what matters here is …

- I get that you really care about …

If you miss the mark, the other party will have the opportunity to correct you, and your incorrect conclusion will prompt her to be explicit about what is important to her. If you hit it on the nose, she will be pleased and reassured. You might notice a smile, a shift toward a more relaxed posture, or eager head nodding. If you haven't already had this experience with co-workers, you will find it very rewarding.

It may be a bit uncomfortable at first, but once you get used to it, you'll wonder why you didn't do this all along. Mastering the art of listening for what's important probably gets you 60% of the way toward becoming more influential.

SKILL #2:
DESCRIBE A ROSY FUTURE

Influence is nearly always about the future: getting approval for a future course of action or building support for specific goals and approaches. Even when you are trying to influence someone to reinterpret the meaning of past events, it's usually part of an attempt to build influence for the future.

But, here, another aspect of geek culture frequently gets in the way, specifically geeks' orientation toward problems and solutions. By their nature, problems are rooted in the here and now. A problem is about a deficiency in the present or an unexploited opportunity. Geeks love a good problem and can't help engaging with a well-constructed, compelling question. But for most non-geeks, problems are uninspiring. They want to be enticed by the prospect of a better future, not to be repelled by a negative present.

What we mean by a rosy future

Imagine that you want to upgrade your company's email server with new, superfast, solid-state storage because the current equipment is slow and will only get worse over time. Typically, you would go to get approval and explain the problem with a statement like:

> "We need to buy this new storage because the current system is slow and will continue to get slower as our data volume grows. As our staff grows, this will only get worse."

Here's the same request but describing a rosy future instead of a looming problem:

> "We would like to buy this new storage in preparation for our staff expansion. We want people to get their email faster and more reliably today and position us to serve our expanding staff with the same high level of service."

Notice the difference? The rosy future emphasizes positive experiences set in the future. The problem emphasizes a flaw in the present that needs to be fixed.

Non-geeks are more likely to be moved by imagining the positive experiences that the new reality will bring. Essentially, it is the difference between pain relief and pleasure seeking. If you want to influence someone, you need to shift your approach toward what will motivate him, rather than what will motivate you.

Describing a rosy future appeals both to people's sense of reason and emotion.

When I hear a compelling vision for the future …	
Reason	I am engaged and start to consider the dependencies for how to get there.
Emotion	I feel good about feeling good in the future, and feel good about you.

Why geeks resist

While shifting your approach to describe a positive experience in the future may seem like a fairly straightforward, easy thing to do, we have found that many geeks struggle with this skill. We have observed that geeks don't like to talk about the future, because it feels like lying. No one really knows what the future will bring, so describing a future as if it were a certainty feels dishonest. And geeks loathe dishonesty. But as long as you realize you're describing a possible future and not promising a particular outcome, you can feel freer to describe a scenario without feeling disingenuous.

How to reframe a problem as a rosy future

Here's an exercise to help you focus your imagination, not on the probable facts of the future, but on the experience and feelings of people in that future.

1. Describe a problem that you'd like to fix at work.
2. Imagine a future where that problem is solved.
3. Imagine the experience of living in that future vividly.
4. Think of a colleague you would like to influence.
5. Write the rosy future for that problem in terms of what that colleague considers important.

Once again, this may feel unnatural at first, but it will become second nature in very short order. You'll be surprised at how much your business partners appreciate this.

SKILL #3: EXPOSE YOUR DESIRE

We've looked at ways to detect and respond to the inner lives of the people you want to influence. This next skill is about exposing your own inner state and telling your partners what it is that's important to you.

At core, this technique is deceptively simple. All you have to do is start a few sentences with the phrase, "I want."

The advantages of this phrase are not obvious at first, and you are not likely to see this skill on anyone else's list of essential soft skills, but it is one of the easiest tools to adopt and one of the most overlooked by people with technical backgrounds.

Why it is important

There are two key reasons that this is so important.

People are suspicious of people with no wants.

Our business partners correctly assume that everyone has desires. And when you don't express yours, they assume that you made a conscious choice to conceal them. And then they become suspicious, because people who conceal their desires often do so for devious reasons, as part of an attempt to gain advantage through concealment or deception.

So when you hide your wants from business partners, they are less likely to trust you and will be less open to your influence. They can't help but think that your advice is secretly self-serving rather than genuine and helpful.

And when you do express your desires, others feel more confident in predicting your behavior because they understand your motivations.

It's easier to come to agreement when everybody is up front about what they want.

When no one is willing to express what they want, progress becomes difficult and conversations stilted.

To get a feel for how important it is to be able to express your desire when trying to influence people, let's look at what happens when desire isn't expressed. Here's an exchange we all might recognize:

ANNA: Where do you want to go for dinner?

BOB: I dunno. Where do you want to go?

ANNA: Well, what are you in the mood for?

BOB: Anything's good for me. I don't really care.

ANNA: How about Chinese?

BOB: I guess, sure.

ANNA: Okay, then I guess we'll get Chinese.

And then our protagonists trudge off to have lackluster dim sum. No desire, no excitement, no shared objectives. They fall into a tenuous same-sidedness by default.

But the dynamic changes radically when desires are expressed.

CARL: Where do you want to go for dinner?

DAPHNE: Hmmm, I'm feeling like something spicy.

CARL: How about that new Szechwan place?

DAPHNE: That sounds great! I'd love to go there!

And now our protagonists bound off, both eager for the heat and spice of a great Chinese meal. Not only did they arrive at their conclusion faster, but they can also be sure that they are less likely to be deterred or distracted by some other option. Expressing their desire cements the fact that they are on the same side in this dinner-getting endeavor.

When you say what you want, it exposes your inner life, reveals what is important to you, gives people a chance to want what you want, and builds trust. Here's how people experience it:

If I know what you want ...	
Reason	I can better predict your behavior. It's a shortcut to agreement.
Emotion	I feel good because we want the same thing and we're on the same side. I feel relieved and can put away my suspicions.

Why geeks resist

Because geeks are so devoted to rationality, logic, and objective truth, they generally believe that subjective things like wants should have nothing to do with decisions at work. In fact, their analytical approach is designed specifically to remove emotional things like wanting from decision-making.

And so, over time, they develop an aversion to expressing their desires at work and even judge those who do as violating some of their common, but unstated, assumptions. Geeks assume that:

Wanting is selfish. People who express their wants at work are self-centered. They prefer to get what they want rather than figure out what's right for everyone involved.

Wanting should be irrelevant. Decisions should be made based on observable facts and logic to maximize the positive outcome for the entire organization. What an individual wants should have nothing to do with decision-making.

Wanting is too risky. And more subtly, expressing wants exposes a person to ridicule, so keeping private wants private is preferable.

How to improve your ability to say, "I want"

When you do express wants at work, they need not be self-centered or selfish. In fact, you probably already do express your wants at work, but disguise them as objective needs rather than personal desires.

Here are a few examples of personal wants that would be easy to express to your business partners:

* "I want this to be the smoothest launch you've ever experienced."

* "I want this new software to make your life easier."

* "I want to protect the students' privacy."

* "I want to give us a competitive advantage, not just keep up."

Experiment with this phrase in low-stakes situations, say at home with your spouse or kids. Our guess is that if you start to say "I want" with people who are not used to hearing you say it, you will notice slightly different, positive reactions from them.

SKILL #4: TRANSLATE FACTS INTO STORIES

Why stories are important for influence

Humans are wired for narrative, from heroic epics to sacred myths to Hollywood blockbusters to bedtime stories to gossip.

The content may change from culture to culture, but storytelling is universal. People generally need to relate to information narratively. Facts aren't enough. Without a cast of motivated characters and a sequence of causal events, facts just float like dust in a spotlight, illuminated but meaningless.

But geeks don't value stories as others do. They tend to think more abstractly. Principles, rules, and frameworks help them to organize facts and give them meaning. That relatively rare ability to think abstractly and manipulate symbols is part of what draws geeks to technical work in the first place. In their work, it's not just an odd quirk, but an essential element of success. But most people need to relate to information as if it were a character in a story.

Some of the most successful IT leaders have a habit of anthro-pomorphizing various aspects of their technology so that non-technical people can get their minds around it. Here's an example from early in Maria's career:

I was planning the feature set for a Web product, and the tech lead kept saying that certain features I requested were "expensive." I asked what he meant by that, and he explained without really changing his metaphor, "When you submit that query, it taxes the system." I listened carefully but never really understood how important that was. And my choices for that product led to our creating something that was, indeed, deathly slow.

Later, the situation was explained to me differently by a tech lead who went on to become a director. He said, "When you submit the query, you are telling it to run through the whole database and look in every row and every column asking, 'Are you there?' That's why, the more data in your database, the more your query has to run around looking under every rock, and it slows the system down. It's very draining." As soon as I could picture the story of a query, I could appreciate the significance of the cost to the system, and I was able to much more easily modify problematic requirements.

Without the story of how the query worked, I heard the information but not the meaning, and didn't change my thinking. With the story, I got the meaning and adjusted my approach. I was influenced by the able tech lead and glad of it.

To become more influential at work, you'll need to hone your ability to translate your native tongue of concept into story.

If I hear facts in the context of a story or metaphor ...	
Reason	I can actually understand what you are saying.
Emotion	I can relate to the meaning of your facts and be stirred to decisive action.

Why geeks resist

Geeks resist telling stories because they mistrust anecdotes. Let's take a minute to look at why that is.

In logic, we are taught that examples are not a form of proof, that anecdotes are not evidence. But here geeks fall into a logical trap of hasty generalization. They apply that rule to all things in life rather than restricting it to reasoning about abstractions. They believe that there are no valid uses for anecdotes.

A more valid conclusion would be to recognize the contextual uses of anecdotes. In many instances, they are helpful vehicles for evidence.

And in case you need evidence for the value of anecdotes and influence, neuroscience is beginning to offer exactly that.

Scientists are now finding that our brains our designed to process information by observing a sequence of causal events. A good story activates mirror neurons in the brain as the listener imagines himself in the story. It triggers cortisol, a hormone associated with focusing attention, and oxytocin, the empathy hormone, which engenders warm, caring feelings.

How to translate facts into story

Since we're all wired for storytelling and narrative, you already have it in you. We don't need to teach you how to tell a compelling story. But we find that translating concepts and symbols into stories doesn't always come naturally. It takes a concerted effort and practice to translate facts, logic, and reason into a narrative structure.

Start with your goal

Think about a situation that you want to influence. Be explicit about what decision needs to be made, the best course of action, who will be making the decision, and what is important to them. Your goal will be to move that person to change what he thinks, feels, or believes in such a way that he makes a decision in support of that action.

Capture the facts

Then simply write down the most important, convincing facts related to your case. For example:

Facts:

* We have 12 help desks on campus.

* Each help desk has its own tracking software and procedures.

- Faculty, staff, and student satisfaction with tech support was found in a survey to be at its lowest point in 10 years.

- The two biggest complaints in the satisfaction survey were that people didn't know which help desk to call or were constantly being bounced from one to another.

- We spend 25% more on support per user than our peer institutions.

Think of an experience

Then think of an experience – real, hypothetical, or even metaphorical – that references these facts, as well as the emotions triggered by the situation. Tell what happened, and what resulted. The story emerges from causal events.

Here's an example of an experience that contains the facts:

Last month the dean of the arts college called me to complain about how much trouble he had getting help with a hard drive problem on his laptop. He couldn't figure out which of our 12 help desks to call, so he just randomly picked one. He waited on the phone for 10 minutes and then was told that he had to call someone else. And as I listened to him, I felt worse knowing that we spent 25% more than our sister institutions, only to give him such poor service.

End with a moral

Make sure there is a "moral" to your story. Be explicit about what your listener should conclude about this story.

Here's the meaning implied by the story:

I really want us to have an easy-to-use, cost-effective help desk system. I think we can save a lot of money if we can just prioritize this project for next quarter.

Formula

And just for kicks, here's a formula for a basic story structure that can contain any kind of fact.

Someone [did | experienced] something that was [surprising | intriguing | unexplained |embarrassing | exciting | difficult | etc.] which led to an outcome that is very [good | bad], and we should do something about it.

Skill #5: Restore trust

Every work relationship has breakdowns eventually. Projects have problems. Expectations aren't met. Or personalities clash.

These breakdowns, if handled poorly, can destroy all of your good work and undermine your influence. At the same time, if handled well, you can recover from a relationship breakdown with more influence than you started with.

When problems arise, geeks tend to focus exclusively on fixing the problem. Unfortunately, no matter how capable you are at fixing technical problems, your business partners will not feel good about you or your technology if you don't manage the feelings that arise with these issues.

In Paul's book *8 Steps to Restoring Client Trust*, he outlined a simple approach for overcoming inevitable conflicts, handling both the facts and the feelings.

1. *Be prepared* – for inevitable breakdowns.
2. *Get the facts* – as your business partner understands them. Just listen.

3. *Find the feelings* – about the situation and the relationship.

4. *Let business partners know you got it* – listen for what's important to them.

5. Dispute the facts (if you must) – but only if it's important.

6. *Frame the problem* – to ensure that the meaning of the problem is not misconstrued or blown out of proportion.

7. *Handle the feelings* – by offering an apology for the facts, the feelings, and the impact of the problem.

8. *Handle the problem* – by fixing whatever went wrong.

Remember, just as empathy is essential in building trust, it is even more important when restoring it.

CONCLUSION

By now, hopefully, you no longer feel that IT leaders can never overcome the persistent influence deficit. They can get the influence that they've been talking about for decades.

But it will take consistent and persistent work on your part to lower the barriers (the resistance) to your influence, as well as practice in the techniques to break through.

Too much is at stake to give up. Technology has become too central to the success of organizations to accept that the folks in technology will forever be relegated to second-class status. Geeks owe it to themselves, to their staffs, and to their organizations to strive for influence commensurate with the technology they oversee.

PART IV

ADDITIONAL INFORMATION

SELLING TO GEEKS

This chapter was originally written to introduce non-geeks to how geeks make buying decisions. It is in Paul's voice and speaks directly to salespeople. We think you will find it useful for two reasons. 1. You'll develop a greater appreciation for what your non-geek colleagues don't know about you. 2. You'll acquire a more formal sense of what your technical colleagues need when making purchase decisions.

Geeks can be tough customers. I should know – I am one.

I've spent 25 years in technology, sitting on both sides of the table, as a geek being sold to, and selling to geeks myself. I've noticed that what makes us so good at what we do – writing code, designing systems, and troubleshooting technical problems – is precisely what makes us such a challenge to sell to.

For non-geeks selling to geeks, we might seem overly cautious, nit-picky, risk-averse and paralyzed by analysis. We don't necessarily laugh at your jokes or talk about our kids. The techniques you use on other people don't work on us. And often, it seems like we just plain don't like you.

And for geeks who are selling to geeks, you may have never systematically examined how people with a technical background approach purchase decisions. You may also have wondered why standard sales techniques often don't work with geeks.

What you need to know, and what I wish everyone who tries to sell me a product or service knew, is:

- Geeks really do see the world differently than most people.

- Though different, geeks are predictable.

- A few slight adjustments to tried-and-true sales strategies will greatly increase the likelihood of your closing important deals with us.

The good news

You'll be glad to know that you don't have to reinvent your sales approach to be more successful in selling to geeks. You merely need to make a few adaptations. This advice is based on the cardinal rule of sales: Know your customer. When you understand how we geeks see the world and how that's reflected in our approach to decision-making, you can win more business and develop productive long-term relationships. More specifically, you need to understand:

- How geeks think

- How we make decisions

- What excites us

- What offends us

- What moves us to act

Let's look at how you need to adapt five of the most common winning sales strategies.

ACCESS EMOTIONS THROUGH REASON

At the core of most approaches to sales is the assumption that buying decisions are ultimately emotional acts. In fact, there's even good scientific evidence that emotions are essential for decision-making. Therefore, it makes sense for you to design your approach to tap into the buying emotions of your customer.

Geeks, like everyone else, need to feel moved to make a buying decision. And yes, we do have emotions despite all evidence to the contrary. But we don't value emotions the same way that other people do. Most people trust their own intuition – their emotionally driven insights of unknown origin – but not geeks. Geeks have emotions and intuition like anyone else, but we prefer to test our intuition rather than trust it.

Geeks value an objectively verifiable reality far above a subjective experience. What that means is that we love observable truth and we scorn the murky world of feelings. While most people feel safe in the world when they share similar feelings with other people, we feel safe in the world because we feel connected to external, dispassionate truth. Ironically, we are rather passionate about dispassionate truth.

When confronted with a decision, our approach is not to search our inner feelings for an answer but to follow a methodical, analytical approach. The purpose of analysis is to remove emotions from the decision-making process. To analyze something, you break ideas down into their constituent parts and test each one independently against an objectively verifiable reality. Then you recombine all of the parts and test them collectively. If they pass muster at each level, then the idea is considered valid.

Once we've analyzed something, we can feel comfortable that our decisions are well reasoned and based on the best information available rather than our subjective experience.

The old saying that "reason makes people think and emotion makes people act" isn't quite right for geeks. It would be more accurate to say that reason makes us think and emotion makes us suspicious. When you try to appeal to our emotion rather than to our reason, we assume that you're trying to distract us from a rational evaluation of your offering. If you're appealing to our emotion, you must think that your product can't stand up under scrutiny.

In sum, trying to tap directly into a geek's emotions elicits a powerful negative reaction. First, we suspect that you're trying to divert our attention away from rational analysis of your offering to try to disguise its weakness. Then we get deeply offended. We take it to mean that you think rather little of our ability to reason. It is as if you are calling us stupid. The result of appealing to our emotion is we lose trust in you as a partner for helping us make decisions.

How to access emotion through reason

You can trigger positive emotional responses from geeks as long as you remember that sound reasoning makes us feel good. Just as bad reasoning or blatant emotional appeals make us feel suspicious and outraged, good reasoning makes us feel safe and satisfied.

What really makes us feel good is solving problems. We find joy in the experience of finding the right answer. While most schoolchildren feel battered and bruised at the end of a hard math question, geeks find a sense of elation. We revel in the discovery of a piece of objective truth, something verifiably correct. For most of us, it's that experience that led us to choose to go into technical work in the first place.

The more you can help geeks to see how your offering solves problems elegantly, the more motivated we will be to accept your offer.

Now let's look closer at what all this means for solution selling.

ARTICULATE CLEAR PROBLEM STATEMENTS, NOT PAIN POINTS

For nearly a generation, people have been taught that they should focus on selling solutions rather than products or services. The model of problem and solution is great for geeks. When it comes to work, and perhaps to everything, geeks see the world through the lens of problems and solutions. In fact, there is little in life that is more motivating to geeks than a problem that needs solving. So if you want to move a geek to action, the best thing you can do is articulate a problem that needs to be solved and provide an optimal solution to that problem.

But the traditional approach to selling solutions is a bit off for geeks. Usually, the first step of selling solutions is to find the customers' "pain points." You've probably learned many ways of uncovering those pain points, such as asking formulaic questions such as, "What keeps you up at night?"

The trouble with this approach is that, as much as geeks love problems, we don't want to choose to address a problem based on something as subjective as anxiety or pain. Remember, geeks don't like to put much stock in emotion. We don't consider it a valid basis on which to make investment decisions. So the traditional question, "What keeps you up at night?" not only is useless with geeks, it's vaguely offensive, implying that we would use emotion as a criterion to judge which problems should be solved.

Of course, in many cases, the answer to the "pain points" question yields the same answer that you get through more rigorous analysis, because most executives have good instincts about which problems are causing the biggest problems for the organization. But if you start with the emotional questions rather than the analytical ones, you're fighting an uphill battle.

That begs the question, what problems do geeks want to solve? If asked, we will tell you that we want to work on the ones that will have the biggest measurable payback to the organization, but that tells only part of the story. We'd answer by describing our preferences for going after low-hanging fruit, where the payback is big relative to a very small investment. Or we might say that we'd tend toward making the biggest possible impact on the organization, investing more to reap larger returns.

A more honest answer would be that we want to work on the most compelling problems we can rationally justify. In other words, though we don't like to admit it even to ourselves, we do allow emotional criteria, our enthusiasm, to creep into our decision-making. But we limit the effect we allow our emotions to have. We won't attack problems that are unjustifiable, but all things being equal, we will put a thumb on the scale of the ones that are most compelling.

Therefore, you need to know a lot more about what makes problems compelling to geeks and how to talk about them to leverage their motivational power.

An example of the power of a good problem statement

A few years ago a potential client called to ask if I could give a motivational talk. He was the CIO of a billion-dollar industrial firm and was hoping I'd come in the following week to address a group of employees and consultants working on a troubled project.

At that moment, I could easily have said yes and taken his money. Had I done so, I would have been accepting the problem statement as, "You want someone to come in to entertain and energize the people on your project." But if you look at the characteristics of a good problem statement, that failed a number of important tests. It didn't identify what was wrong with the situation or what the impact was. It didn't provide any measurable value. And also, it offered a solution to an unidentified problem.

After some discussion, it became clear that his concern was that the team was failing to meet its deadlines due to lack of motivation. That caused me to modify the problem statement to, "Your project team is missing deadlines, and you want someone to come in to give a presentation that will help motivate them."

But that still failed a number of important tests. It didn't identify the root cause of the team's lack of motivation, or the impact. It still didn't provide any measurable value. And also, it offered an implausible solution to the problem. Just giving an uplifting speech wouldn't solve the underlying issues with the project that were the source of the team's mood.

I told him that I wasn't comfortable taking his money, since it wasn't clear that giving a motivational talk would deliver any value. But we continued talking. After probing him about the history of the project, it became clear that the team lacked motivation because they believed that the project was going so badly that it would be canceled. But from talking to the CIO, I knew he had no intention of canceling the project and was committed to getting it back on track. Finally, I was able to propose a problem statement that I thought would work.

"Basically, what you really need is to get your $2 million, mission-critical software development project completed by the end of July and the team committed to its success."

At that, he let out an excited, "Yes!"

Once we agreed on the problem statement, we could discuss more appropriate solutions. Instead of giving a motivational talk, I ended up consulting for the team over the next year. Not only was it more helpful to the client, but it was more lucrative for me.

How to articulate a motivating problem statement

Instead of searching for the emotionally determined pain point, help geeks describe their needs in the form of a motivating problem statement.

Crafting motivating problem statements is the single most important thing you can do to close more business with geeks.

What is a problem statement?

Problem statements mean so much to us geeks because they perform a critical organizing function in our thought process. Since we love math, which is structured by problems, we have come to rely on problem statements in all aspects of life.

For us, problem statements transform the unstructured ambiguity of everyday life into something sufficiently concrete for us to deal with. Without a problem statement, we feel adrift and unsure of what we're supposed to be doing. We can't know what the right answer is without a clearly defined problem, and that leaves us uneasy. We feel deeply the need to know that there is a right answer, because we desperately dislike being wrong. Simply put, problem statements describe how it is possible for us to win.

There is a fair amount of leeway in what we consider to be problem statements, since it's more about their function and less about their specific form. Ironically, they may contain neither a problem nor a statement. They may focus on:

Issues. A description of what's wrong with the current situation. "Our customer satisfaction numbers are terrible because our help desk response times are twice as long as they should be for Level I calls."

Opportunities. A description of opportunities that we want to exploit. "Using video chat during our Level I help desk calls will increase customer intimacy and improve our customer satisfaction scores."

Objectives. A set of objectives that we want to achieve. "We want to improve our customer satisfaction numbers this quarter by reducing our response times by 20%."

Method questions. A question about how we might improve the current situation, exploit an opportunity, or achieve a set of objectives. "How could we improve our average customer satisfaction score from 3 to 4 in the next six months?"

In any given situation, you can frame a problem statement a number of different ways. Before selecting one formulation over another, you need to think about how it will sound to your prospect. For example, statements about issues may sound to your customer like an indictment of their competence and trigger defensiveness, which is probably not helpful in sales conversations.

What a problem statement is not

As a geek being sold to, I've noticed that there are three common ways that salespeople try to highlight problems that always fall flat. I think this is because they lack the understanding of how we think and talk about problems. Here's what I wish they knew:

A fact is not a problem. The simple statement of a fact without context is not a problem. For example, a salesperson might say, "Your average customer satisfaction score was 3 last month," with a look of urgency on his face. My response? "So what?" When I hear this, it makes me think that the person trying to sell to me is either too lazy to want to understand my problems or too stupid to know that a disconnected fact is meaningless to me.

The absence of a solution is not a problem. I have a similar response when someone frames my problem as the absence of some sort of solution. This happens frequently when someone's trying to convince me to upgrade to a newer technology. "You really need a new payroll package." Really? Why? This isn't a problem statement at all but a proposed solution to an unarticulated problem. It may be true, but my real problem would be something like, "Your vendor is going to discontinue support for your current payroll package, making maintenance difficult and expensive."

The absence of a benefit is not a problem. The last of the most common mistakes of problem framing is defining my problem as the absence of a benefit. "You need to lower the cost of running your payroll." Really? I might. But from this statement, I don't know if my payroll costs are out of line for the industry, if they're bankrupting the company, or if they're already the lowest in town. And even if it is a problem, there might be something else that's much more important for me to focus on.

How to create a motivating problem statement

Now that you know how important problem statements are to geeks and what they are and aren't, let's get specific about how you can craft a problem statement that is irresistible to geeks. There are three features of problem statements that can make them compelling.

- The clarity they provide
- The value that solving them yields
- The fun of problem-solving itself

If there ever was a perfect problem statement, it was uttered on May 25, 1961, by President John F. Kennedy.

"I believe that this nation should commit itself to achieving the goal, before this decade is out, of landing a man on the moon and returning him safely to Earth. No single space project in this period will be more impressive to mankind, or more important in the long-range exploration of space; and none will be so difficult or expensive to accomplish."

It galvanized a generation of scientists and engineers to change the course of human history. Let's keep it in mind as we look more closely at the elements of what makes problem statements compelling.

Clarity

Good problem statements provide clear information about what we're trying to accomplish. For geeks, that clarity is a prerequisite for motivation. Without it, there is virtually no chance that we're going to be eager to make decisions. To make a problem statement clear, it needs to be:

Foundational. Good problem statements get to the heart of the matter rather than focusing on minutia or distractions. They identify the core issues to be addressed and the impacts of the issues. They point out the costs of the existing problems and the benefits of resolving them.

Brief. Compact problem statements draw attention to precisely the issues that need to be addressed. Long, rambling statements are ambiguous and frequently result in teams solving the wrong problem or being unable to evaluate options and choose a course of action.

Specific. Specificity in a problem statement provides readers with the scope that their solution needs to address. It helps teams avoid the trap of trying to solve too many problems at once or of coming up with overly narrow approaches that are insufficient.

Non-prescriptive. Problem statements define what opportunity is to be exploited or what deficiency addressed. They do not specify the approach to solving the problem.

Measurable. In some cases, but certainly not all, problem statements define the measures by which a solution should be judged. Some problems are more quantifiable than others. But don't fall into the trap of assuming that unmeasurable things are unimportant. Often, they're the most important of all.

By these standards, Kennedy's problem statement is exceptionally clear. When he challenged us to land a man on the moon and return him safely to Earth by the end of the decade, it was brief, specific, measurable, and non-prescriptive. If you were an engineer at NASA at that time, you knew exactly where the goalposts were.

Value

As with most people, geeks can be highly motivated to work on a particular problem because the results are important. This may be measured by something objectively verifiable like monetary impact. For example, "Optimizing your inventory levels will save the company $10 million a year." But it also may be more personally meaningful. For example, "Your senior management will recognize how important you are in keeping this place running if they're not distracted by the help desk's low customer satisfaction scores."

Looking back at Kennedy's statement, he created a deeply felt sense of importance by referring to what achieving the goal would mean to mankind and tapping into the dream of space exploration.

Just plain fun

But whether or not geeks find the results of solving a problem compelling, we can get excited simply by the prospect of solving the problem itself. We choose technical work because we find grappling with big, thorny problems rewarding. We not only get the sense of satisfaction and excitement that comes from solving them, but we enjoy the process that leads to the solution. There are a number of things that can make a problem interesting to tackle. These include:

Degree of difficulty. Easy problems are boring. Difficult problems are intriguing. Impossible ones are infuriating. Since problem statements tell us the rules of the game we're playing, you can use them to highlight the difficulty of the problem to make it interesting. The easiest way to do this is by including constraints that put the problem in the sweet spot of difficulty, not too easy and not too hard.

Learning new things. Most geeks love learning new things, especially if we think that those things will be useful in the future. If solving a problem requires learning to use new technology, that can be a real inducement. If it requires learning some ancient tool that no one will ever use again, it can be a real turnoff.

Competition. You may not think of geeks as being competitive, but we can be very competitive with one another. If others have failed to solve the problem, that makes the challenge much more enticing. It may not be the noblest of motives, but we do like proving that we deserve to be high up in the geek hierarchy. I doubt you'll ever explicitly call this one out in a problem statement, but you don't have to. We'll know what you mean.

4 Ways to Make a Problem Statement More Motivating

Basic Statement: How can we reduce the costs of software testing while improving its effectiveness?

Value	Difficulty	Learning	Competition
How can we reduce the costs of software testing while improving its effectiveness, *to lower the cost of post-release support by reducing the call volume by 10%?*	How can we reduce the costs of software testing while improving its effectiveness *in time to test the June 1 release of the product?*	How can we reduce the costs of software testing while improving its effectiveness *by adopting the most up-to-date testing methodology and tools?*	How can we reduce the costs of software testing while improving its effectiveness to make our June 1 release *the highest-quality software the company has ever introduced?*

And once again, Kennedy's problem statement shines by touching on all of these. Nothing could be more difficult or unprecedented than going to the moon. He even manages to get that into the statement itself. Of course, the most compelling motivation was competition with the Soviet Union, but he wisely left that one unspoken.

CLARIFY *HOW* BENEFITS ARE ACHIEVED

Sales wisdom says that you need to focus on benefits. To motivate people to buy, you need to focus more on how your offering helps them than on how it works. And your experience probably bears this out. Most people don't want to hear long descriptions of the detailed features of your product or service. Most people don't want to know what process you follow or detailed specifications of your product. They just want to know what good it will do.

But geeks won't buy into *what* your product or service accomplishes unless they understand *how* it does so. In short, geeks don't trust your benefits claims. Until proven otherwise, your benefit statements are presumed to be fantasies or lies. We need to see an explicit link between the features of your product or service and the benefits that you claim it offers before we'll even consider buying it.

Recently I was helping a client purchase invoicing software that could automate unusually complex calculations. In my search, I found that nearly every company's focus on benefits was so overwhelming that it was impossible to tell what the product actually did. Each website displayed nearly identical lists of benefits: more accurate invoices, faster billing, reduced labor cost, more flexible terms. But no matter how far I dug into their sites, I couldn't tell anything about how the product actually worked.

None of them told me anything about whether they could be configured for specific requirements, by what means they interface with other systems, what sorts of parameters they supported, or whether they could handle international currencies. They all seemed to think that a mere promise of benefits was all that was required to get my interest. I just became frustrated and predisposed to think that they were bozos and their products were crap.

But conventional wisdom isn't entirely wrong. Geeks do want to know about benefits; they just need to know more.

How to make your benefits believable

When you're selling to geeks, you need to show in detail how the features of your offering solve the problem that you agreed to work on together. You can think of it as a three-step proof.

1. Craft a clear problem statement.
2. Demonstrate how the benefits of what you're selling resolve the problem.
3. Show how the features of your offering directly deliver the benefits.

Once you've shown these links, you've established yourself as a plausible source for a solution and made your geek customer much happier to be working with you.

It's not that geeks have an insatiable desire to examine the details of your product or service. It's that the details are required for us to believe that you can solve our problem.

Note the importance of the aforementioned problem statement. If we haven't agreed on what problem we're trying to solve, we really have no interest in your product's features, because we don't even know if we need those benefits. And benefits can only be evaluated in the context of how they relate to an explicitly described problem.

As an example, consider what those invoicing software companies could have done to encourage my interest rather than annoy me. My problem statement would have been something like, "We need to automate the calculation of our invoices outside of our accounting package to improve accuracy and reduce labor costs."

Therefore, the benefit statements on the front pages of the invoice software company websites were a perfect fit for what I was looking for. I would have been happy to contact them had they provided just a little more information about how their product worked and what their capabilities were. I didn't want to waste time calling two dozen companies just to find out a few basic facts about their products. All they needed to tell me on the website was whether their software was capable of interfacing with the existing accounting package, handling international currencies, and supporting rule-based calculations on imported data.

At that stage of the sales process, I didn't need to know every detail of how the product worked. But before purchasing, I probably would.

BUILD RAPPORT BY FOCUSING ON WORK

Everyone knows that people buy from people they like, so you need to work on building a personal connection with your prospects. Believe it or not, geeks do appreciate personal connection.

We value personal relationships, but in a work context you need to earn the right to become personally familiar. We tend to be introverts and don't find personal connection rewarding for its own sake, especially when the motives of the person wishing to connect with us are not purely personal. In this environment, we open up to relationships slowly as you earn trust and credibility through the work we do together.

If you overemphasize personal connection during the sales process, geeks become suspicious that you are trying to distract us from a rational evaluation of your offering. We get insulted if it looks as if you're trying to convince us to buy something because we like you personally. To us, it feels like you're saying that we are so dumb that we can be manipulated easily.

This response is fairly easy to trigger. When I used to manage a large group of software development consultants, salespeople would call up all the time to invite me to lunch to talk about what their products could do for us and our clients. Occasionally, I would say yes, but only if I was genuinely interested in the products.

As a geek, the invitation by itself wasn't that appealing. I didn't really crave the fine dining or the opportunity to meet someone new. So when we met, I was primarily interested in learning about the products. But usually, the salespeople would launch into familiar conversation, probing for personal details that seemed completely irrelevant to me. "I've got three kids. How about you?" I found these questions jarring and intrusive. I had agreed to meet to learn about a product, not to discuss my family life. After I get to know someone, I might be more interested in exploring whether we share hobbies or have vacationed in the same places. Their attempts to be prematurely familiar was uncomfortable and off-putting and diminished the likelihood that I would want to do business with them.

How to build rapport with geeks

You should try to build rapport with geeks while working to define problems and proposed solutions. Geeks connect with others through work rather than outside it. Don't try to build rapport in the sales process by asking personal questions about hobbies or personal history. We are likely to think of you as smarmy and self-serving. To geeks, these questions are beside the point, since they don't fit into the model of problem or solution.

But once you've worked together for a while and established the relevance and credibility of your products and services, once you've proved yourself as someone who is able and willing to work through problems and solutions collaboratively, you'll have earned the right to ask personal questions and connect in a less formal manner. Be patient and earn our trust first.

MANAGE RISK, DON'T JUST HANDLE OBJECTIONS

One of the core skills you might have learned as a salesperson is how to handle customer objections. You've studied a variety of techniques for dealing with complaints and concerns that block or delay deals. And just like everyone else, we geeks need you to handle our objections when they come up. We expect you to respond to our concerns, to know your product or service, and to be able to stand up to aggressive questioning.

But if you passively wait for issues to come up, you miss a huge opportunity to speed up the sales process and earn personal trust. That's because most salespeople don't understand how we think about risk management and conflate it with objections. For geeks, these are completely separate things.

Traditional objection handling is a fundamentally defensive act that carries with it negative feelings. You're supposed to prepare yourself to defend your product and positions, convince customers that their concerns are either unfounded or insignificant, or diminish the emotional intensity of their objections by explaining that all customers feel this way at some point in the process. It's like being hunkered down in a foxhole with a small arsenal at your side. Every time a prospect throws an objection at you, you have to pick which weapon provides the best defense. Do you try to block the objection? Do you counterattack? Do you try to take it and hurl it back at the customer yourself?

Risk management, on the other hand, is a proactive and enjoyable activity. For us, it's more than just a habit of thought. We consider it our sacred obligation. Whenever there are unknowns, whenever there is uncertainty, we feel duty-bound to understand the situation as best we can. We do it instinctively whenever there's an important decision to be made. In the sales context, we engage in risk management in order to ensure that we are prepared to get the benefits of your offering. By doing this, we build confidence that we can avoid or prepare for any obstacles that might undermine our success.

How to manage risks

Loosely speaking, risk management has two parts: risk identification and risk planning. First, you figure out all of the unknowns that might have an effect on the project or operations. Then, you plan what to do in order to minimize the chance that it will happen or minimize the impact should it happen.

When you encounter geeks in the sales process who are doing risk management, it feels like they are working hard to scuttle your deal by imagining every possible objection and hurling them at you rapid fire. Some of them are pretty ordinary "what if" questions that you hear every day. But others seem bizarre and unlikely. For example, if you were selling software-testing services, we might ask you questions like:

- How do you handle staffing when you have multiple projects with the same deadline?

- How do you handle knowledge transfer when you lose key people?

- What sort of redundancy do you have if there's a natural disaster at your primary location?

If you handle these questions as if they were objections rather than explorations of risk, you're likely to alienate geeks, since taking a defensive stance during risk management leads to us to believe that you're trying to hide something rather than help us analyze the suitability of your offering. Our natural response is to assume that the information you're providing is itself an unknown, a risk to be managed, and that means you have to be treated with suspicion. In short, treating risk management as objection handling undermines any trust that you've already earned.

As someone who frequently sells to geeks, I know that the way I engage with my client's sense of risk can make or break a deal. I remember one client who seemed as if he wanted to move ahead on a project, but still was feeling a bit uneasy about the risks involved. He continued bringing up "what if" scenarios, asking how we would handle them should they arise.

Eventually, he came up with one so obscure that it never even occurred to me before as something that was possible. Instead of trying to come up with some sort of clever response on the spot, I decided to give him an open and honest answer. I said, "I've never really considered that possibility before, so honestly I don't know how we would handle it. Were that to happen, we would have to sit down together, examine the circumstances and the options, and work something out. I'm confident that between us, we'd be able to come up with some good options."

And then I gave him an example of how I had handled unforeseen problems that occurred with another client and collaborated to work through the issues. I could see his face change as we discussed it further. He became more relaxed and comfortable with the decision as he found out about the philosophy underlying our approach to dealing with unforeseen circumstances and as he saw that I was committed to collaborative problem-solving rather than avoiding blame. Shortly thereafter, we signed a contract and began the project.

Some salespeople think that they earn our trust by pointing out minor weaknesses of their product. They believe that small disclosures will convince us that they are providing full disclosure and unbiased information. Real estate agents use this technique all the time by pointing out a worn spot in the carpet in hopes that you won't notice the giant hole in the roof. We know the difference between an insignificant annoyance and a deal-killing flaw. Proactive disclosure only works with geeks if you're pointing out the biggest risks involved. We're not that gullible or easily convinced that we don't need to think for ourselves.

5 Do's and Don'ts for Managing Risk in Sales

DO learn to recognize the differences between genuine objections and questions about risks.

DO proactively participate in risk management rather than avoiding it and hoping it will be unnecessary to close the deal.

DO volunteer information about the problems that come up most often when implementing your product or working with your clients on projects.

DON'T pretend problems never happen. Instead, explain how you handle them when they arise.

DON'T worry about bursting our bubbles or undermining our fantasies that you are the perfect vendor with an unimpeachable record. We don't believe anyone who says that they don't have problems.

Rather than trying to obviate our need to do risk management, participate in it freely. The more we geeks feel that you are a reliable partner in performing the necessary analysis, the more we will trust you. The more defensive you are in the process, the more you undermine that trust.

BONUS: HOW GEEKS SHOW EXCITEMENT

And finally, you need to know that geeks express enthusiasm quite differently than other people. In fact, the times when we are most enthusiastic about your offering are probably the moments when you feel that we are being most negative and critical. The opposite is usually true. We don't bother analyzing things we're not interested in. If we are genuinely enthusiastic about something, we invest the time and energy to really examine it, to confirm that our enthusiasm, our subjective experience, is justified by objectively verifiable facts. When we're tearing apart your product, trying to figure out how it won't work, it's a really good sign. Don't look for big smiles and quickened pulses. Our level of interest and excitement is in direct proportion to the intensity of our scrutiny.

CONCLUSION

Increasingly, geeks are involved in purchasing decisions within organizations. Whether they are decision-makers or influencers, you need to understand how to sell to them.

When you learn to recognize how the archetypal geek thinks and makes decisions, you can adapt your approach to improve your results. You'll feel more powerful and less frustrated, thwarted, and confused. You can help geeks feel safe in choosing you and your products or services by respecting the need to verify your benefits and analyze their risks. You can earn their trust by appealing to reason rather than emotion.

The more you understand geeks, the better prepared you will be to influence these tough customers and win more business.

ABOUT THE AUTHORS

PAUL GLEN is the founder of the Leading Geeks Company. He has spent more than 25 years working on technical projects, leading technical organizations, and helping technical leaders. Since 1999, he has poured his energy into improving the quality of technical leadership as a consultant, author, and presenter.

His previous book, *Leading Geeks: How to Manage and Lead People Who Deliver Technology*, won several awards. Among them was the 2003 Financial Times Germany International Book Prize, as the best new book published worldwide on the subject of leadership. Since 2003, he has written a column for *Computerworld*, for which he was awarded a 2007 National Silver Medal for Editorial Excellence by the American Society of Business Publication Editors.

He received an MBA from the J.L. Kellogg Graduate School of Management at Northwestern University, with majors in marketing, organizational behavior, and strategy. His BA is from Cornell University, with majors in computer science and mathematics. He has also taught as an adjunct faculty member in the MBA programs at Loyola Marymount University and the Marshall School of Business at the University of Southern California.

MARIA MCMANUS, a partner at Leading Geeks, spent her career at the intersection between technical, creative, and business people on digital development teams, as a pioneer and leader in user experience strategy and design. As a vice president of the first-generation Internet success iVillage and as a director of user experience at Disney Interactive Media Group, Maria accepted it as her calling to bridge the gap between these different types of people in order to create better products more efficiently.

In 2011, Maria officially joined Paul to help establish Leading Geeks as the premier voice in promoting geek/non-geek understanding.

Having studied English and American literature at Brown University and Mount Holyoke College, Maria's attention to the nuances of subjective experience, highlighting common threads and subtle differences, has significantly shaped the insights of this book.

ABOUT

LEADING GEEKS

The Leading Geeks Company helps organizations unlock the value of technical people by overcoming the disconnect between technical and non-technical groups. That includes:

- Launching project teams on a path to success

- Redirecting troubled projects, with attention to repairing critical relationships

- Improving technical leadership, by recognizing that leading geeks is different from leading non-geeks

- Transforming the tricky relationships between technology and business groups

Since 1999, Leading Geeks has empowered leaders to leverage technology and the people who provide it.

Today, Paul Glen and Maria McManus, the founding partners, bring a unique perspective to improving collaboration across disparate organizational cultures. They leverage their decades of experience from opposite sides of the chasm to uncover overlooked ways of getting along, thereby enhancing organizational productivity.To find out more about how Leading Geeks might help you, contact info@leadinggeeks.com.

GET HELP

The Leading Geeks Company helps organizations unlock the value of technical people through consulting, coaching, educational programs, keynote presentations, and publishing.

To learn more and explore how Leading Geeks may be able to help in your organization:

- Download free white papers: http://www.leadinggeeks.com/publications/free-downoads

- Learn about Leading Geeks' customizable keynotes and workshops: http://www.leadinggeeks.com/keynotes

- Read Paul Glen's award-winning books and *Computerworld* column at: http://www.leadinggeeks.com/publications

REFERENCES

Abee, John. Bringing Minds Together. Harvard Business Review. July – August, 2011.

Adler, Paul; Heckscher, Charles; and Prusak, Laurence. Building a Collaborative Enterprise. Harvard Business Review. July – August, 2011.

Akinbode, I. Adefolu, and Clark, Robert. A Framework for Analyzing Interorganizational Relationships. Human Relations. Vol. 29, No. 2, 1976.

Amabile, Teresa M. "Creativity and Innovation in Organizations." Harvard Business School, 1996.

Amabile, Teresa M. "How to Kill Creativity." Harvard Business Review, September – October, 1998. 76-87.

Amabile, Teresa M. "Managing for Creativity." Harvard Business School, 1996.

Amabile, Teresa M. "The Motivation for Creativity in Organizations." Harvard Business School, 1996.

Argyris, Chris. Teaching Smart People How to Learn. Harvard Business Review. May – June, 1991.

Assael, Henry. Constructive Role of Interorganizational Conflict. Administrative Science Quarterly. Vol. 14, No. 4, December 1969.

Banker, Rajiv D.; Hu, Nan; Pavlou, Paul A.; Luftman, Jerry. CIO Report Structures, Strategic Positioning, and Firm Performance. MIS Quarterly, Vol. 35 No. 2, June 2011.

Barki, Henri, and Hartwick, Jon. Interpersonal Conflict and Its Management in Information Systems Development. MIS Quarterly. Vol. 25, No. 2, June 2001.

Baron Cohen, Simon, The Essential Difference: Male and Female Brains and the Truth about Autism. New York: Perseus Book Group, 2003.

Beckwith, Harry. Selling the Invisible: A Field Guide to Modern Marketing. Warner Books, 1997.

Beer, Michael; Eisenstat, Russel A.; and Spector, Bert. Why Change Programs Don't Produce Change. Harvard Business Review. November – December 1990.

Bennis, W. On Becoming a Leader. Reading, MA: Addison-Wesley, 1989.

Bennis, W., and Biederman, P.W. Organizing Genius: The Secrets of Creative Collaboration. Cambridge, MA: Perseus, 1997.

Brooks, F.P. Jr. The Mythical Man-Month: Essays on Software Engineering. Reading, MA.: Addison-Wesley, 1975.

Brown, Karen A.; Ettenson, Richard; and Hyer, Nancy L. Why Every Project Needs a Brand (and How to Create One). MIT Sloan Management Review. Vol. 52, No. 4, Summer 2011.

Budzier, Alexander. Why Your IT Project May Be Riskier Than You Think. Harvard Business Review, Vol. 89 No. 9/10, September – October 2011.

Burley-Allen, Madelyn. Listening: The Forgotten Skill. John Wiley & Sons, 1995.

Capretz, Luiz Fernando. Personality types in software engineering, International Journal of Human-Computer Studies, Volume 58, Issue 2, February 2003.

Castor, Theresa, and Cooren, Francois. Organizations as Hybrid Forms of Life. Management Communication Quarterly. Vol. 19, No. 4, May, 2006.

Cialdini, Robert B. Influence (rev): The Psychology of Persuasion. HarperCollins, 1993.

Cooper, Randolph B. The Inertial Impact of Culture on IT Implementation. Information & Management. Vol. 27, No. 1, July 1994.

Corwin, Ronald G. Patterns of Organizational Conflict. Administrative Science Quarterly. Vol. 14, No. 4, December 1969.

Crawford, Lynn, and Brett, Christine. Exploring the Role of the Project Sponsor. Proceedings of the PMI New Zealand. 2001.

Cross, Rob, and Thomas, Robert. A Smarter Way to Network. Harvard Business Review. Vol. 89, No. 7/8, July – August 2011.

Csikszentmihalyi, M. Finding Flow: The Psychology of Engagement with Everyday Life. New York: Basic Books, 1997.

Davidson, Richard J., and Begley, Sharon. The Emotional Life of Your Brain: How Its Unique Patterns Affect the Way You Think, Feel, and Live – and How You Can Change Them. Penguin.com, 2012.

Dvir, Dov, and Shenhar, Aaron J. What Great Projects Have in Common. MIT Sloan Management Review. Vol. 52, No. 3, Spring 2011.

Ekman, Paul. Emotions revealed: Recognizing faces and feelings to improve communication and emotional life. Macmillan, 2007.

Fairhurst, Gail T., and Sarr, Robert A. The Art of Framing. Jossey-Bass, 1996.

Fiol, C. Marlene; Pratt, Michael G.; O'Connor, Edward J. Managing Intractable Identity Conflicts. Academy of Management Review. Vol. 34, No 1, January 2009.

Gardner, H. Leading Minds: An Anatomy of Leadership. New York: Basic Books, 1995.

Gemmill, Gary. The Dynamics of the Group Shadow in Intergroup Relations. Small Group Research. Vol. 17, No. 2, May 1986.

Gillespie, Nicole, and Dietz, Graham. Trust Repair After an Organizaition Level Failure. Academy of Management Review. Vol. 34, No. 1, January 2009.

Gino, Francesca, and Pisano, Gary P. Why Leaders Don't Learn from Success. Harvard Business Review. April 2011.

Gladwell, Malcolm. Blink: The power of thinking without thinking. Hachette Digital, Inc., 2007.

Grandin, Temple, and Sean Barron. "Unwritten rules of social relationships: Decoding social mysteries through the unique perspectives of autism." Future Horizons, 2005.

Greene, Joshua. Moral Tribes: Emotion, Reason, and the Gap Between Us and Them. Penguin, 2013.

Hagel, John 3rd, and Brown, John S. Productive Friction: How Difficult Business Partnerships Can Accelerate Innovation. Harvard Business Review. Vol. 83, No. 2, February 2005.

Hertz, Paul, and Dowse, Chris. Does CIO Behavior Derail Intentions? CIOInsight. May 2009.

Hertzberg, Frederick. "One More Time: How Do You Motivate Employees?" Harvard Business Review, September – October 1987. 6-13.

Humphrey, W.S. Managing for Innovation: Leading Technical People. Englewood Cliffs, NJ: Prentice-Hall, 1987.

Humphrey, W.S. Managing Technical People: Innovation, Teamwork, and the Software Process. Reading, MA: Addison-Wesley, 1997.

Jameson, Jessica K. Toward a Comprehensive Model for the Assessment and Management of Intraorganizational Conflict: Developing the Framework. International Journal of Conflict Management. Vol. 10., No 3, July 1999.

Katzenbach, J.R., and Smith, D.K. "The Discipline of Teams." Harvard Business Review, March – April 1993. 111-120.

Keltner, Dacher. Born to be good: The science of a meaningful life. WW Norton & Company, 2009.

Kenrick, Douglas T., and Griskevicius, Vladas. The rational animal: How evolution made us smarter than we think. Perseus Books Group, 2013.

Kesner, Idalene F., and Fowler, Sally. When Consultants and Clients Clash. Harvard Business Review. November – December 1997.

Kidder, T. The Soul of a New Machine. New York: Atlantic-Little, Brown, 1981.

Kim, W.C., and Mauborgne, R. "Fair Process: Managing in the Knowledge Economy." Harvard Business Review, July – August 1997. 65-75.

Lam, Tham, and Lau, Teresa. Evidence on Efforts to Align Organizational Structures and Business Strategies. Global Journal of Business Research. Vol. 4, No. 1, 2010.

Lehrer, Jonah. How we decide. Houghton Mifflin Harcourt, 2009.

Leidner, Dorothy, and Kayworth, Timothy. Review: A Review of Culture in Information Systems Research: Toward a Theory of Information Technology Culture Conflict. MIS Quarterly. Vol. 30, No. 2, June 2006.

Lerner, Jennifer S., and Dacher Keltner. "Beyond valence: Toward a model of emotion-specific influences on judgement and choice." Cognition & Emotion 14.4, 2000. 473-493.

Levin, Daniel Z.; Walter, Jorge; and Murnighan, J. Keith. The Power of Reconnection – How Dormant Ties Can Surprise You. MIT Sloan Management Review. Vol. 52, No. 3, Spring 2011.

Levinson, Harry. "Asinine Attitudes Toward Motivation." Harvard Business Review, January – February 1973. 70-75.

Levy, S. Insanely Great: The Life and Times of Macintosh, the Computer That Changed Everything. New York: Penguin Books, 1994.

Linzmayer, O. Apple Confidential: The Real Story of Apple Computer, Inc. San Francisco, CA: No Starch Press, 1999.

Lorsch, J.W., and Mathias, P.F. "When Professionals Have to Manage." Harvard Business Review, July – August 1987. 78-83.

Luftman, Jerry, and Brier, Tom. Achieving and Sustaining Business-IT Alignment. California Management Review. Vol. 42, No. 1, Fall 1999.

Luftman, Jerry, and Kempaiah, Rajkumar. An Update on Business-IT Alignment: "A Line" Has Been Drawn. MIS Quarterly Executive. Vol. 6, No. 3, September 2007.

Maister, D.H. Managing the Professional Service Firm. New York: Free Press, 1993.

Maister, D.H. True Professionalism: The Courage to Care About Your People, Your Clients, and Your Career. New York: Free Press, 1997.

Mangelsdorf, Martha E. How Too Much Multitasking at Work Can Slow You Down. MIT Sloan Management Review. Vol. 52, No. 3, Spring 2011.

McCarthy, J. Dynamics of Software Development. Redmond, WA: Microsoft Press, 1995.

McConnel, S. After the Gold Rush: Creating a True Profession of Software Engineering. Redmond, WA: Microsoft Press, 1999.

McConnell, S. Code Complete: A Practical Handbook of Software Construction. Redmond, WA: Microsoft Press, 1993.

Merrill, David W. Personal styles and effective performance. CRC Press, 1981.

Mintzberg, H. "Covert Leadership: Notes on Managing Professionals." Harvard Business Review, November – December 1998. 140-147.

Morieux, Yves. Smart Rules: Six Ways to Get People to Solve Problems Without You. Harvard Business Review, Vol. 89, No 9/10, September – October 2011.

Peery, Newman, Jr. Technical Rationality and Political Behavior Within Organizations. Academy of Management Proceedings. August 1975.

Phillips, Nelson; Lawrence, Thomas; Hardy, Cynthia. Inter-Organizational Collaboration and the Dynamics of Institutional Fields. Journal of Management Studies. Vol. 37, No. 1, January 2000.

Pondy, Louis R. Varieties of Organizational Conflict. Administrative Science Quarterly. Vol. 14, No. 4, December 1969.

Prasad, Jayesh; Enns, Harvey G.; Ferratt, Thomas W. One size does not fit all: Managing IT employees' employment arrangements. Human Resource Management, Vol. 46, No. 3, Fall 2007.

Quinn, J.B.; Anderson, P.; and Finkelstein, S. "Managing Professional Intellect: Making the Most of the Best." Harvard Business Review, March – April 1996. 71-80.

Raelin, J.A. The Clash of Cultures: Managers Managing Professionals. Boston: Harvard Business School Press, 1991.

Rahim, M. Afzalur. A Strategy for Managing Conflict in Complex Organizations. Human Relations. Vol. 38, No. 1, 1985.

Reich, Blaize Horner, and Benbasat, Izak. Factors That Influence the Social Dimension of Alignment Between Business and Information Technology Objectives. MIS Quarterly. Vol. 24, No. 1, March 2000.

Ren, Hong; Gray, Barbara. Repairing Relationship Conflict: How Violation Types and Culture Influence the Effectiveness of Restoration Rituals. Academy of Management Review. Vol. 34, No. 1, January 2009.

Rizzo, John R.; House, Robert J.; and Lirtzman, Sidney I. Role Conflict and Ambiguity in Complex Organizations. Administrative Science Quarterly. Vol. 15, No. 2, June 1970.

Schein, E.H. Organizational Culture and Leadership. San Francisco, CA: Jossey Bass, 1992.

Schein, Edgar H. On Dialogue, Culture and Organizational Learning. Organizational Dynamics. Vol. 22, Issue 2, Autumn 1993.

Sosa, Manuel E.; Eppinger, Steven D.; Rowles, Craig M. Are Your Engineers Talking to One Another When They Should? Harvard Business Review. Vol. 85, No. 11, November 2007.

Sweetman, Kate. Embracing Uncertainty. MIT Sloan Management Review. Vol. 43, No. 1, Fall 2001.

Tomkins, Silvan S. Affect, imagery, consciousness: Vol. I. The positive affects. 1962.

Tomlinson, Edward, and Mayer, Roger C. The Role of Causal Attribution Dimensions in Trust Repair. Academy of Management Review. Vol. 34, No. 1, January 2009.

Turner, Arthur N. Consulting Is More than Giving Advice. Harvard Business Review. September – October 1982.

Tusman, Michael. Apolitical approach to organizations: a review and rationale. Academy of Management Review. April 1977.

Twomey, Daniel. Interorganizational Conflict Resolution: The Effects of Power and Trust. Academy of Management Proceedings. Meeting Abstract Supplement, August 1975.

Van den Steen, Eric. On the Origin of Shared Beliefs (and Corporate Culture). MIT Sloan Working Paper 4553-05, August 2005.

Van den Steen, Eric. Organizational Beliefs and Managerial Vision. MIT Sloan Working Paper 4224-01, July 2001.

Van den Steen, Eric. The Limits of Authority: Motivation versus Coordination. MIT Sloan Working Paper 4626-06, August 2006.

Walsham, Geoff. Cross-Cultural Software Production and Use: A Structural Analysis. MIS Quarterly. Vol. 26, No. 4, December 2004.

Walton, Richard E., and Dutton, John M. The Management of Interdepartmental Conflict: A Model and Review. Administrative Science Quarterly, Vol. 14, No. 1, March 1969.

Walton, Richard E.; Dutton, John M.; and Cafferty, Thomas P. Organizational Context and Interdepartmental Conflict. Administrative Science Quarterly. Vol. 14, No. 4, December 1969.

Weinberg, G.M. Becoming a Technical Leader: An Organic Problem-Solving Approach. New York: Dorset House Publishing, 1986.

Weinberg, G.M. The Psychology of Computer Programming. New York: Van Nostrand Reinhold Company, 1971.

Weinberg, G.M. Understanding the Professional Programmer. Boston, MA: Little, Brown, 1982.

Wray, K. Brad, ed. Knowledge and Inquiry: Readings in Epistemology. Broadview Press, 2002.

Xie, Jinhong; Son X. Michael; and Stringfellow, Anne. Interfunctional Conflict, Conflict Resolution Styles, and New Product Success: A Four-Culture Comparison. Management Science. Vol. 44, No. 12, December 1998.

Zirpoli, Francesco, and Becker, Markus C. What Happens When You Outsource Too Much? MIT Sloan Management Review. Vol. 52, No. 2, Winter 2011.

ACKNOWLEDGEMENTS

The insights included in this book were hard won, and this book would not exist were it not for the contributions of some very important people.

We would like to thank Kyle Shannon for his early, ebullient support of this topic and for helping us to structure the conversation in a way that moves people. Without his input, this work would not have happened.

We would also like to thank our friends at Citrix Online. Their dedication to providing technical leaders with genuinely useful information challenged us to create content that was more relevant and actionable than it would have been otherwise. Veronica Puailoa, Todd Lewis, James New, Katelyn de Diego, Jessica Brown, and Shabana Siyed have been a delight to work with.

Jamie Eckle gets double appreciation. As the editor for Paul's *Computerworld* column, Jamie expressed enthusiasm for the first hints of our geek/non-geek insights and has served as a most excellent editor for this book. His editorial judgment as well as his dedication to clarity, precision, and readability benefit writers and readers alike.

Our friends at EDUCAUSE were also essential for making this book happen. They offered us the opportunity to test, clarify, and refine the ideas in this book with hundreds of higher-education technical leaders from all over the country who enriched us with their wisdom. We are grateful for the ongoing support of Lida Larsen, Julie Little, and Teddy Diggs.

Many other exemplary geek leaders in their own right have made real contributions to this conversation. We are particularly grateful to Vicki Milledge, Lucas McGregor, Joe McGrath, Michael Hugos, Dan Galorath, Eric Fanzon, and Linda Cureton.

And closer to home we would like to thank Cashel McManus O'Malley, a perceptive 16-year-old whose questions and challenges pushed us to more clarity. And special thanks go to Ernie Glen, a delightful 10-year-old and future geek leader who surprised and inspired us again and again.